T0383929

Master Incapable

Master Incapable
无能子

A Medieval Daoist on the Liberation of the Mind

Translated by
Jan De Meyer

OXFORD
UNIVERSITY PRESS

Oxford University Press is a department of the University of Oxford.
It furthers the University's objective of excellence in research, scholarship,
and education by publishing worldwide. Oxford is a registered trade mark of
Oxford University Press in the UK and in certain other countries.

Published in the United States of America by Oxford University Press
198 Madison Avenue, New York, NY 10016, United States of America.

© Oxford University Press 2023

Library of Congress Cataloging-in-Publication Data
2023915082

ISBN 978-0-19-760327-7

Printed by Sheridan Books, Inc., United States of America.

Contents

Acknowledgments

The author wishes to express his gratitude to Marianne Bujard (École Pratique des Hautes Études) and to Carine Defoort and Benedicte Vaerman (KU Leuven) for their help in making available certain hard to find sources.

Introduction

Overview

Master Incapable is an important but relatively little-known Daoist text written in 887 (the third year of the Guangqi reign period), as the Tang dynasty (618–907) was breathing its last. When compared with the bulk of Tang-dynasty Daoist literature, *Master Incapable* immediately stands out. Almost entirely free of Buddhist or Confucian influence, and not focused at all on the themes ubiquitous in most Tang Daoist texts (such as immortality and how to attain it), *Master Incapable* takes us straight back to the fountainhead of Daoist thought. Indeed, it is in the Daoist classics—*Laozi* 老子, or the *Daodejing* 道德經 (*Scripture of the Way and Its Power*), *Zhuangzi* 莊子 and *Liezi* 列子—that Master Incapable finds the tools with which to fashion his own vision of the world.

And a radical vision it is! Master Incapable begins by recounting his story of how humanity—the "naked creature"—separated from the natural world, and eventually found itself drowning in its own blood. He has very outspoken opinions about what he judges to be the pernicious role of the intellect, worldly ambitions, emotions, and cravings, and he even dares to claim that emperors are only emperors because they can dispose of certain material attributes, implying a very serious criticism of the theory of the Heavenly Mandate (*tianming* 天命), in which heaven confers the emperor (the "Son of Heaven," *tianzi* 天子) with the right to rule, though this right will be lost if the ruler behaves in dissolute and immoral ways. He also indicates how mankind may escape from its predicament: by being spontaneous or natural (*ziran* 自然), by engaging in nonpurposive action (*wuwei* 無為), and by freeing oneself from intentionality and desire (*wuxin* 無心, *wuyu* 無欲), all important elements of Daoist thought. That *Master Incapable* has long been neglected is probably due to its being such a late Masters Text (*zishu* 子書), coming so many centuries after the first and best-known period of Masters Literature—from the fifth through the third century BC—came to an end.[1] Yet there can be no doubt as to its unique position in the history of Daoism, and in the intellectual history of the Tang dynasty.

As a philosophical work that develops the radical tendencies of *Zhuangzi*'s so-called "primitivist" chapters and the proto-anarchist views

---

1   On Masters Texts, see Denecke 2010 and Denecke 2017.

of the early fourth-century Bao Jingyan 鮑敬言, *Master Incapable* stands unchallenged in its virulent attacks on conventional standpoints: those concerning life and death, body and spirit; the perceived differences between the human and the animal realms; language and intelligence; human emotions and aspirations.[2] Fiercely egalitarian in tone, it criticizes superstition from a rationalist and naturalist standpoint, and it offers a coherent philosophy of reclusion. Despite the radical nature of *Master Incapable*'s philosophy, the book even found admirers among some princes of the Ming dynasty (1368–1644), who reprinted *Master Incapable* along with other Tang-dynasty philosophical works.[3] As a work of literature, it combines forcefully argued discussions and alternative takes on well-known historical episodes with glimpses into the private life of the philosopher, his family members, and his entourage. Its powerful, concise, and unadorned language may also be considered typical of ninth-century "ancient-style prose" (*guwen* 古文).[4] A discussion of the philosophy, literariness, and linguistic features of *Master Incapable*, as well as its historical context, will serve as the main focal points of this introduction.

Superficially, the name "Master Incapable" has a pejorative ring to it, suggesting that its owner felt powerless to devise solutions to the seemingly insurmountable problems of his own day and age, or worse, that he had no abilities whatsoever. In an attempt to explain the choice of pseudonym, Gert Naundorf quotes the Yuan-dynasty poet and official Liu Yin 劉因 (1249–1293) to remark upon an old Daoist tradition of presenting oneself as ignorant or lacking refinement.[5] "A gentleman of consummate virtue has an appearance that makes him look ignorant," writes Sima Qian 司馬遷 (c. 145–c. 86 BC) in his biographical sketch of Laozi, and the *Daodejing* itself states: "My mind is that of an ignorant man . . . Ordinary men look bright and astute, I alone look dim-witted and benighted."[6] It is, however, not at all necessary to interpret the pseudonym "Incapable Master" as pejorative. Both in *Liezi* and in *Zhuangzi*, including Guo Xiang's 郭象 (252–312) *Zhuangzi* commentary, we find

2   For a more detailed treatment, see p. xxii.
3   See Wang 2012, 75–76. The texts *Master Incapable* accompanied includes such works as *Master Kangcang* (*Kangcangzi* 亢倉子), *The Master of Mysterious Realization* (*Xuanzhenzi* 玄真子), and *The Master of Heavenly Seclusion* (*Tianyinzi* 天隱子).
4   I return to this topic on p. xxix.
5   Naundorf 1972, 21–23.
6   For the quote from *Records of the Historian* (*Shiji* 史記), see the chapter "Discourse on Sun Deng" at the end of Book II. The second quote is from *Daodejing* 20.

several instances of "incapable" that lend the pseudonym a much more positive connotation.[7]

Chapter 20 of *Zhuangzi*, for instance, contains a conversation between Confucius, who is being besieged and is afraid of dying, and an old man who informs Confucius about a way to stay alive. The old man talks about a bird that looks utterly incapable of anything (*wuneng*)—it cannot even fly without the help of others—but is never harmed by other beings. And in chapter 32 of *Zhuangzi*, "Uncle Dim Nearblind" reflects on "those who are incapable" (*wunengzhe* 无能者) in the following terms: "Labors beset the skillful and worries beset the wise, but those without any abilities are free of all seeking: they eat until they're full and then they wander around aimlessly, drifting like an unmoored skiff. Empty and aimless, they wander."[8] Also in the first *Liezi* chapter, we find a passage that may have inspired the choice of the pseudonym "Master Incapable."[9] *Liezi*'s argument is that that which makes things into what they are—it is described as the "responsibility of nonpurposive action"—is itself as endless, as timeless, and as intangible as the Way (*dao* 道).[10] The same *Liezi* passage concludes by describing the Way-like "responsibility of nonpurposive action" as being devoid of knowledge and utterly incapable, "and yet there is nothing which it does not know, and nothing of which it is incapable."[11] Thus, from a Daoist perspective, the epithet "incapable" is actually a phrase of only seemingly counterintuitive praise, as *wuneng* is a synonym for being unharmed, remaining free and unfettered, and even a characteristic of

7   In the Han dynasty (202 BCE–220 CE), *Zhuangzi* consisted of fifty-two chapters. By the end of the third century, that number had been cut to thirty-three. Some of the *Zhuangzi* text that was excised wound up in Guo Xiang's commentary to the new *Zhuangzi*, other fragments found a home in *Liezi*, an originally pre-Han Daoist work probably no longer extant by 300. See Littlejohn 2011. For more on Guo Xiang and Zhuangzi, see Robinet 1983.
8   Ziporyn 2020, 260.
9   Yang 1985, 10.
10 *Wuwei* 無為, though literally meaning "non-action," is best translated as "non-assertiveness," "non-intervention," "nonpurposive action," or "effortless action." Edward Slingerland has explained this seeming paradox of "effective" "non-action" like this: "it refers to the dynamic, effortless, and unselfconscious state of mind of a person who is optimally active and effective. People in *wuwei* feel as if they are doing nothing, while at the same time they might be creating a brilliant work of art, smoothly negotiating a complex social situation, or even bringing the entire world into harmonious order." Slingerland 2014, 7.
11 The translation is in Graham 1960, 20.

the functioning of the Way, it is not necessary to picture *Master Incapable*'s author as a helpless creature convinced of his inability to offer any remedies against the evils of his time.[12]

As for that author, we do not know who wrote the text; whoever he was, he chose to remain hidden behind the pseudonym Wunengzi 无能子, "Master Incapable." From the preface accompanying the book we can infer that *Master Incapable*'s author once occupied an official position, which he relinquished at the time of the devastating rebellion led by Wang Xianzhi 王仙芝 and Huang Chao 黄巢 (875–884), a failed examination candidate turned salt smuggler. We also know that he had a number of disciples, and that, when he wrote his book, he lived in poverty in the commoner's house of a certain Mr. Jing 景氏 in the capital region.[13] But knowing when the book was written is enough to offer some insight into what the anonymous author was responding to in *Master Incapable*.

The Times

When *Master Incapable* was being prepared for inclusion in the *Complete Library of the Four Repositories* (*Siku quanshu* 四庫全書), it received a notice dated 1781, the latter part of which reads:

> The *Tang Treatise on Literature* takes this book to be the work of someone who went into reclusion among the populace during the Guangqi reign period. When examining the preface, we read about "no mention being made of the author's name or his official career." Therefore the author could not have been someone who went into reclusion among the populace. The book has pilfered many of its ideas from *Zhuangzi* and *Liezi*, which it intersperses with Buddhist sayings. The wording and opinions are quite superficial. Only because remaining works from the Tang dynasty have now become scarce

---

12 This is from Guo Xiang's *Zhuangzi* commentary, which repeatedly posits *wuneng* as an essential trait of the workings of the Way. In his commentary to *Zhuangzi* 17, for instance, Guo Xiang states that "he who understands the *dao*, knows that it is 'devoid of abilities' (*wuneng*)." As it is devoid of abilities, it cannot be held responsible for the creation of individual beings, because the Way is itself nothing but the principle of autonomous creation (Guo Qingfan 1985, 588).

13 Poverty is a frequently recurring theme in *Master Incapable*, written at a time when institutionalized inequality had reached an apex. In the first half of the eighth century, an imperial prince received tax revenue from ten thousand households. According to a 709 report to the throne, a group of 140 aristocrats received income from no less than 54 prefectures, which amounted to about 15 percent of the entire empire (see Benn 2002, 20).

do we accept it for the time being, as it is an old edition, which we
continue to rank amongst the Daoists.[14]

With almost palpable disdain, the Confucian writer of the notice detects
only one quality in *Master Incapable*: the fact that it is old and belonging
to a period with a very low survival rate for literary works. Even though
the work is accepted into the largest collection of books in all of Chinese
history, it is only done so "for the time being" (*gu* 姑), as if the compilers'
magnanimity might be anything but lasting.

Thanks to the preface attached to *Master Incapable* we are unusually
well informed about the date and composition of the work. The preface,
which was probably written by the author himself, states: "During the
daytime, he liked to lie in bed without sleeping. Lying there, he would fill
a few sheets of paper with writing. When he got up, he would keep them
close to his chest without showing them to me. Between the *renshen* day
of the second spring month and the *jihai* day of the final spring month, he
filled a few dozen sheets of paper, which he rolled up and put in a bag."
Master Incapable was thus composed between March 26 and April 22 of the
year 887, at a time when the Tang dynasty was in full decline.[15] In order to
fully appreciate the steepness of the decline, as well as the radical nature of
Master Incapable's critical analysis of what he considered was wrong with
the times, it is necessary to present a short overview of the Late Tang and
some of its ailments.

The Tang is often presented somewhat simplistically as consisting of
two halves: a period characterized by a strong centralized government,
military expansion, economic growth, and a tremendous cultural blos-
soming; and a subsequent downward spiral, weak rulers, and a steadily
increasing decentralization of power. The caesura in Tang history is the An
Lushan Rebellion (755–763), which, with an estimated loss of more than
ten million lives, was in many ways highly traumatic. However, its impact
cannot be compared to that of the Huang Chao Rebellion 120 years later,
which brought the dynasty to its knees.

The final demise of the Tang dynasty in the first years of the tenth century was the result of a great number of partially interrelated factors.[16] The
enormous empire, which stretched from present-day Korea in the northeast

14 See Ji Yun et al., rpt. 1986, vol. 1059, 550.
15 This information is so detailed and precise that only the author of *Master Incapable*
    himself could have written the preface. Who else would have known what Master Inca-
    pable did in bed during those four weeks? Unless, of course, the author of the preface
    was Huayangzi, Master Incapable's "bodily friend."
16 The following sketch of the gradual decline of the Tang is largely based on Peterson 1979,
    464–560; Dalby 1979, 561–681; and Somers 1979, 682–789.

and Vietnam in the south to the Pamir Mountains in the west, was too large to manage. The heavily militarized frontier zones had long been managed by military governors (*jiedushi* 節度使), but in the wake of the An Lushan Rebellion military regions were also installed in the interior, with some regions led by former rebel leaders who had been amnestied. In these territories the court lost much of its grip on the tax system, and henceforth the fertile valleys of the lower reaches of the Yangzi River would be the state's chief source of tax income. In regions where a part of the original population had died in warfare or moved away, the state tried to compensate for the loss of tax revenue by increasing taxes on the remaining inhabitants, which gave them a reason to emigrate. The state support of the Buddhist clergy—a formidable economic power around the year 800—also put a very heavy strain on the government's finances, which led to a major repression in 845, whereby thousands of Buddhist monasteries and shrines were destroyed or desacralized and more than a quarter of a million monks and nuns were forced to return to a life of productive labor and tax paying.[17] From the third and fourth decades of the ninth century onwards, popular uprisings were numerous, even in the relatively prosperous southeast.

In the fall of 859, a new emperor was put on the throne by eunuchs, after his capable and well-respected predecessor died following experimentation with Daoist life-prolonging elixirs. Posthumously known as Yizong, he would be remembered as the least worthy of all Tang rulers. He amused himself with excursions accompanied by a retinue of thousands, and cared more for Buddhist than state matters. He replaced high officials from families who had been known for their active support of the dynasty with eunuchs or his personal favorites. Against official protest, he appointed a musician as general of the palace guard in 867.[18] When Yizong gave one of his daughters in marriage to a protégé, he donated an extraordinary amount of money and an estate to the young couple. When the princess died only one year later, the emperor had the more than twenty physicians who had treated her executed, and officials who dared criticize this cruelty were eliminated. The Buddhist cremation ceremony for the princess became "notorious as one of I-tsung's most unbridled acts of imperial extravagance."[19] When the emperor died in 873, two eunuchs put his eleven-year-old son on the throne. One understands better why Master Incapable would fulminate against rulers being able to elevate commoners to the highest positions

17 See Ch'en 1956.
18 See Twitchett 1979, and Sima Guang 1972, 8118.
19 Somers 1979, 710.

simply by "enforcing names," as in the chapter "Discourse on Yan Ling" in Book II (see p. 65).

Meanwhile, parts of China had been seriously shaken by more popular unrest. The Huang Chao rebellion began in 875 in Shandong province and was joined by farmers driven to despair by droughts, floods, locust infestations, failed crops, famine, bureaucratic corruption, and excessive taxation. Taking his army to the deep south, Huang Chao destroyed Guangzhou, killing perhaps more than half of its two hundred thousand inhabitants, then returned north to occupy the capitals of Luoyang and Chang'an in the winter of 880. While young emperor Xizong fled to Sichuan in the west, Huang Chao founded his own dynasty, the Qi 齊 (meaning "equality," but also referring to Shandong province).

In 881, troops loyal to the Tang assembled in the capital region, but few generals dared to attack Huang Chao's army. Late in 882 the court asked the Shatuo 沙陀 Turks for assistance and managed to drive Huang out of Chang'an with an army led by a former companion of Huang's, ending his reign of terror in the spring of 883. After four years in exile, in early 885 Emperor Xizong returned to the ruins of Chang'an, but almost all of Chinese territory was now held by Tang generals, former rebel leaders, or Turkish troops. Fighting continued—as stated in the preface to *Master Incapable*—and less than a year after his return, Xizong was forced to flee once again. In 888 he returned to Chang'an one last time, where he died at the age of twenty-six, never having truly ruled.

Huang Chao's destruction of the capital region proved to have far more serious long-term effects compared to the already disastrous An Lushan Rebellion. The great aristocratic clans that had dominated medieval China for centuries were annihilated, and their disappearance forever altered China's power structure.[20] The warfare that Master Incapable witnessed in 887 would continue for many decades. The Tang was officially declared defunct in 907 and the Chinese territory entered a new period of division, known as the Five Dynasties and the Ten Kingdoms. It would take the newly founded Song dynasty (960–1279) another nineteen years to conquer the Northern Han, ruled by a clan of Shatuo Turkish ethnicity, and finally reunify all of China in 979.

Tang-dynasty Daoism

The Tang has been called "the most significant period in the history of Daoism, because it was then that the religion showed that it could satisfy the spiritual, cultural and political needs of the entire society."[21] Tang-dynasty

---

20 On this topic, see Tackett 2016.
21 Kohn and Kirkland 2000, 339.

Daoism was an extremely complex phenomenon, as it was the result of a millennium of growth and development. Its roots were the philosophical writings attributed to the shadowy figures of Laozi (dates unknown) and Zhuangzi (ca. 369–286 BC). The *Laozi*, or *Daodejing*, is a short text presented as counsel to a ruler to extend his rule by using techniques that may seem to go against everyday logic, such as refraining from taking purposive action so as to guarantee that "nothing remains undone" (*wu bu wei* 無不為).[22] The ruler should be like water or a newborn child and embody virtues such as flexibility or softness, because soft overcomes hard and hardness is a sign of death approaching. *Zhuangzi* is quite diverse in tone: many different voices can be heard in its styles, and some chapters treat civilization as a disease while others offer a synthesis of basic Daoist tenets and Confucian values.[23] The biggest difference with the *Daodejing* is that *Zhuangzi* is relatively unconcerned with how the empire is to be governed. Indeed, the general advice offered is to steer clear of politics, and it is in *Zhuangzi* that we find the first coherent philosophy of what we call "reclusion" or "eremitism," namely the refusal of power, and the avoidance of shortening one's natural lifespan by being greedy, ambitious, or simply useful to mankind. But the *Daodejing* and *Zhuangzi* share the same basic values such as that of *ziran*, literally "so-of-itself," which we usually render as "spontaneity" or "naturalness." Both classics also hint at the possibility of lengthening one's lifespan, which enabled the ideal of immortality or transcendence (*xian* 仙), with separate origins as old as the fourth century BC, to merge with Daoist thought and practice.[24]

22 The text of about five thousand characters was originally in two chapters, scriptures on "The Way" and "Its Power," but was at some point subdivided into eighty-one paragraphs or verses (large portions of the text rhyme and are thus poetry).

23 *Zhuangzi* now consists of thirty-three chapters, the first seven of which are traditionally attributed to the historical Zhuang Zhou 莊周. Some chapters were written by a "primitivist" author, others by disciples who expand on ideas presented in the first seven chapters.

24 The concept of immortality evolved from a belief in the possibility of keeping the body intact for many centuries into a set of theories and practices concerning the formation of an immortal embryo that could rise up to heaven as the physical person died. A multitude of methods, including diet, sexual hygiene, certain forms of meditation and alchemy, were thought to lead towards this post-mortem immortality. Alchemy itself evolved from "external"—ingesting elixirs, the ingredients of which were mostly minerals or metals—to "internal," whereby the human body itself becomes the crucible wherein the vital energies may be refined. Immortals were thought to reside in mountain ranges such as Kunlun 崑崙 in the west and blessed isles like Penglai 蓬萊 in the ocean east of China. Already in the second half of the fourth century BC, kings of the eastern coastal state of Qi organized expeditions in order to find the islands of the immortals.

During the third and second centuries BC, a form of Daoism called Huang-Lao 黃老 (in reference to the Yellow Emperor, Huangdi, and to Laozi), became part of the philosophical mainstream. The word from which our "Daoism" evolved—*daojia* 道家 or the "family of the Way"—dates to the second century BC, when historians and bibliographers started to inventory the Masters Texts in the imperial library, labeling different but related texts under headings we still use today. For the birth of Daoism as a mass movement we have to wait until the second century CE. Tradition has it that a certain Zhang Ling 張陵, also known as Zhang Daoling 張道陵, experienced a vision of the deified Laozi, who selected him to create a new covenant between mankind and the Daoist heavens.[25] The new teaching was called "Covenant with the Powers of Orthodox Unity" (*Zhengyi mengwei* 正一盟威), and Zhang Daoling has since been known as the first Celestial Master (*tianshi* 天師). The movement is known both as "Zhengyi Daoism" and as the "Way of the Celestial Master" (*Tianshidao* 天師道). Under Zhang Daoling's grandson, Zhang Lu 張魯, Daoist communities often known as "parishes" (*zhi* 治) developed into what has been described as a theocratic kingdom, in what is now Sichuan province. Followers were instructed in the teachings of the *Daodejing*, together with a commentary said to have been written by Zhang Lu. They provided their parish with an annual tax of five pecks of rice, and organized "charity lodges" for the indigent. Blood sacrifice was forbidden, and priestly functions were open to men and women. In 215 these communities were forced to leave their original power base, and as a result the Way of the Heavenly Master started to be disseminated throughout the entire Chinese empire. Today most Daoist priests are non-celibate and still identify as followers of the original Zhengyi teachings.

For centuries to come, the history of Daoism would be closely linked to a series of revelations.[26] The first is called Highest Clarity (Shangqing 上清), denoting a corpus of scriptures revealed to a medium working for an aristocratic family in the lower Yangzi region. Highest Clarity Daoism was a synthesis of ancient ecstatic religious traditions, adaptations of elements of the Celestial Master teachings, and immortality-seeking practices. Its scriptures, heavily influenced by old mythology and the writings gathered in the *Verses of Chu* (*Chuci* 楚辭), were of the highest literary quality, and became very popular with the medieval literary elite. Its practice was individual and stressed visualization and meditation. About the year 400, another important corpus of scriptures would be revealed, this time to

---

25 On Zhang Daoling and Celestial Master Daoism, see Pregadio 2008, 981–986.
26 For an introduction, see Pregadio 2008, 663–669, 858–866.

a grandnephew of Ge Hong 葛洪 (283–343), author of *The Master Who Embraces Simplicity* (*Baopuzi* 抱朴子).[27] Known as "Numinous Treasure" (*Lingbao* 靈寶), the new revelation would incorporate much Buddhist material, and the liturgy described in these texts would form the basis of later Daoist ritual, the influence of which can still be felt today.

Well before the Tang dynasty, Daoism had evolved into a multifaceted phenomenon with philosophical and religious dimensions, individual as well as communal practices, and followers in all strata of society. Daoist scriptures, both revealed and not, dealt with a multitude of topics: life-prolonging practices, divination and numerology, alchemy, botany, medicine and pharmacology, sacred history and geography, liturgy, rituals and rules for believers, visualization and meditation, mystical poetry and sacred incantations.

Though no new revelations occurred in the Tang dynasty, the various Daoist traditions then merged into a pyramidal structure. The basis of the structure was formed by the Way of the Celestial Master. All members of the Daoist clergy, about one third of whom were women, started out at this level. Through study and practice it was possible to rise in the ranks of the Daoist hierarchy. Initiation and ordination were linked with the transmission of parts of the Daoist canon. An intermediate level was formed by the Lingbao scriptures, and at the pinnacle stood the hyperliterate tradition of Highest Clarity.[28]

Daoism was omnipresent in virtually every aspect of Tang life. To the rulers of the Tang, surnamed Li 李, the state cult of Laozi was largely ancestral in nature, as the imperial clan considered themselves descendants of Laozi, whose real name was said to have been Li Er 李耳 or Li Dan 李聃. Right from the inception of the Tang, Daoism legitimized the dynasty, since it was Wang Yuanzhi 王遠知 (528–635), a Highest Clarity patriarch, who transmitted the mandate to rule to Li Yuan 李淵 (r. 618–626), the future founder of the Tang.[29] Most Tang emperors sponsored Daoism, though none so energetically as Emperor Xuanzong (r. 712–756), the longest-reigning of all Tang sovereigns. He established Daoist temples throughout the empire, oversaw the compilation of the first veritable Daoist canon, en-

---

27 *The Master Who Embraces Simplicity* consists of twenty "inner" chapters, which focus mainly on immortality, alchemy, meditation and other religious practices, and fifty "outer" chapters, dealing with a great variety of learned topics, such as education, government, history, and personal development. The final chapter is Ge Hong's autobiography.

28 For these aspects, see, among others, Schipper and Verellen 2004, 22–26, Barrett 1996, and Benn 1991.

29 See the entry on Wang Yuanzhi in Pregadio 2008, 1021–1022.

couraged the study of the Daoist classics—he himself wrote commentaries
to the *Daodejing*—and surrounded himself with Daoist advisors. All Daoist
priests and priestesses were granted the status of relatives of the imperial
clan, and the emperor himself was ordained as a Daoist priest. The philos-
opher-priest who oversaw the ordination, the great Sima Chengzhen 司馬
承禎 (647–735), was asked by the emperor to provide the calligraphy for
three different stone engravings of the *Daodejing*, symbolizing the perennial
value of the Daoist classic, which in 747 was declared the most eminent of
all classics. Vast quantities of Daoist writings from the Tang were lost in the
warfare of the late ninth and the tenth centuries, or as a result of the Mongol
ban on Daoist books of 1281. Yet what has survived is still impressive both
in extent and richness, with the continuing influence of the *Daodejing* and
Zhuangzi in evidence nearly everywhere.[30]

One important development in Daoist mysticism was the early Tang
trend known as the "Twofold Mystery" (*chongxuan xue* 重玄學). Borrowing
heavily from Buddhist Madhyamika philosophy, it adapted the analytical
method known as the *tetralemma* to the context of Daoist thought. Using
this method, one moves from an "affirmation of being" to an "affirmation
of nonbeing," and hence to an "affirmation of both being and nonbeing,"
culminating in a "negation of both being and nonbeing." The name "Twofold Mystery" derives from the first paragraph of the *Daodejing*, which
mentions the "mystery within the mystery" (*xuan zhi you xuan* 玄之又玄),
interpreted here as a means of surpassing all contradictions in one's ascent
to mystical union with the Way.

One of the most prolific Daoist authors of the Tang was the aforementioned Sima Chengzhen, who temporarily left his reclusive mountain retreat
when Tang emperors such as Xuanzong solicited his services at court.[31]
Among other works, Sima Chengzhen authored the "Discourse on the
Quintessence of Absorbing Qi" (*Fuqi jingyi lun* 服氣精義論), an important
work on respiratory techniques; the "Plan of Heavenly and Earthly Palaces
and Residences" (*Tiandi gongfu tu* 天地宮府圖), on sacred geography; and
the exquisitely illustrated hagiography of the immortal Wangzi Qiao 王子

30 Aside from Emperor Xuanzong's commentaries on the *Daodejing*, the Ming dynasty
   Daoist canon preserves similar works written by Li Rong 李榮 (7th c.), Li Yue 李約
   (early 9th c.), Qiang Siqi 強思齊 (9th c.), Zhao Zhijian 趙志堅, Lu Xisheng 陸希聲
   (fl. 889–904) and Du Guangting 杜光庭 (850–933), among others. A very important
   surviving subcommentary on *Zhuangzi* is that by Cheng Xuanying 成玄英 (fl. 650). For
   an introduction, consult the first volume of Schipper and Verellen 2004, esp. 283–629.
   On Cheng Xuanying's *Zhuangzi* commentary, see Yu 2000. A number of important Tang
   dynasty texts on Daoist mysticism have been translated in Kohn 2010.
31 For an introduction to Sima Chengzhen, see Kirkland 2008, 911–914.

喬.[32] Sima Chengzhen's name is also connected with the already mentioned "Master of Heavenly Seclusion" and the "Discourse on Sitting in Oblivion" (*Zuowang lun* 坐忘論), two major eighth-century mystical treatises.

Equally rich and important is the literary legacy of the reclusive poet and Daoist priest Wu Yun 吳筠 (d. 778).[33] The fiercely anti-Buddhist Wu Yun wrote mystical poetry, eulogies on hermits, rhapsodies (*fu* 賦) on a great variety of themes (reclusion, bamboo, anti-Buddhism, and the ascent to mystical union with the Way), a treatise on the possibility of studying spirit immortality (or spiritual transcendence, *shenxian* 神仙), and the "Mystic Mainstay" (*Xuangang* 玄綱), an outline of Daoist thought and practice in thirty-three short chapters, presented in 754 to the aging Emperor Xuanzong.

Xuanzong's reign ended in total chaos, with the rebellion of the Turkish-Sogdian general An Lushan (c. 703–757), and while Xuanzong is often blamed for losing his grip on government matters, two factors are singled out for special mention in this context: the emperor's infatuation with his favorite concubine Yang Guifei (719–756), and his overly enthusiastic support of Daoism. In the second half of the Tang, however, imperial support of Daoism continued as before. In Daoist thought, a move away from Buddhist-inspired mysticism is noticeable in favor of a renewed search for an accommodation with Confucianism.[34]

Strikingly anti-Confucian and presenting a radical elaboration of elements of the *Daodejing*, *Zhuangzi*, and *Liezi*, but without being significantly influenced by Buddhism, *Master Incapable* is somewhat of an exception in the intellectual life of the Tang dynasty. Its theory on the human body being fundamentally dead (see Book I, "Analyzing the Delusion" and "Being Free of Worries") sets it apart from Daoists like Wu Yun, who stressed the importance of an equal cultivation of body and mind in the realization of immortality. Although Master Incapable at times refers to Daoist longevity techniques such as grain abstention, the whole "immortality complex," so visibly present in the works of most Tang Daoists, is absent in his text. One

---

32   The best study of the immortal Wangzi Qiao is Bujard 2000.

33   The most complete studies to date of Wu Yun are De Meyer 2006 and Boutonnet 2021.

34   This trend is visible in the philosophical commentaries on the *Daodejing* by the aforementioned Qiang Siqi and Lu Xisheng, and in some of the works of the extremely prolific Daoist author Du Guangting. The most systematic and thorough synthesis of Daoist and Confucian philosophy is Luo Yin's 羅隱 (833–910) "Book on the Identity of Both" (*Liangtong shu* 兩同書), written at about the same time as *Master Incapable*. On the "Book on the Identity of Both," see De Meyer 1992–1993. See also Schipper and Verellen 2004, 298–299; Franciscus Verellen is erroneously credited with the authorship of this introduction, which was actually written by this translator.

wonders whether Master Incapable had any ties with the institutionalized Daoism of his day, beyond his thorough understanding of the *Daodejing*, *Zhuangzi*, and *Liezi*. *Master Incapable*'s voice is unique, and that particular nature is explained in greater detail in the following section.

The Text

Master Incapable is a relatively short text of about 9,500 characters, divided into three books. Its contents are well organized. The first book expounds a theory of the decline of mankind, expressed most forcefully in its first and longest chapter, "The Fault of the Sages." The same chapter also contains some remarkable observations regarding intellect and speech among animals. Other themes in Book I include: the crucial role of naturalness or spontaneity (*ziran*) and nonpurposive action or nonintervention (*wuwei*); the true nature of life and death; the illusory nature of wealth, status, and reputation; the harmful role of emotions; and the absence of intentionality, also known as "no-mind" (*wuxin*).

The second book chooses a different form to cover some of the same ground as the first. It consists of imaginary recreations of dialogues between historical figures, presented in chronological fashion, starting with the future first Zhou king and his advisor Lü Wang 呂望 (11th c. BC), and ending with the third-century hermit Sun Deng 孫登 and the poet and philosopher Xi Kang 嵇康 (223-262). We also meet King Wu of the Zhou 周武王, Laozi, Confucius and some of his disciples, Fan Li 范蠡 (536-448 BC) who was advisor to the king of Yue 越, the writers Song Yu 宋玉 (third century BC) and Qu Yuan 屈原 (c. 339–c.278 BC), four hermits well known in the early Han dynasty, and the recluse Yan Guang 嚴光 (ca. 39 BC–41 CE), an old friend of the first Eastern Han emperor. The leading theme in Book II is societal engagement, and it is a major Tang-dynasty statement on reclusion, as every dialogue is between a hermit (or someone presented as a hermit) and a person active in politics or society.

Central to the third book are Master Incapable's personal experiences. Again, dialogue, mostly between Master Incapable and his friends and family members, as well as with the people Master Incapable lived among while in hiding, occupies an important place. Topics covered include the absence of intentionality, poverty, the question of whether or not to serve in government, the right conduct and refinement, and the lure of alcohol. Master Incapable proposes a naturalist critique of superstition and a radical philosophy of language. Book III also contains parables involving fish changing into dragons and a snake and a poison bird.

Recurring themes in all three parts are: human suffering and its causes, the potentially destructive role of the intellect, the limitations of language (which harbors the first germs of violence), and the functioning of the mind. As Master Incapable posits that there was once a time without rulers and subjects, and that this evolutionary stage was to be preferred over the hierarchical society of later times, it is only logical that historians of Chinese political thought with an interest in anarchism should become interested.[35] However, when *Master Incapable* is mentioned in works on Chinese anarchism, it is often with a tone of frustration or regret, as the text's message seems to move away from what scholars of anarchism would like to have discovered in it.[36] To better understand *Master Incapable*, we should perhaps avoid using labels such as "anarchist."

While on a theoretical level it is possible to agree that "Taoist thought is supremely anarchistic," Daoism in practice has seldom displayed any revolutionary or anti-statist tendencies.[37] Its "program of moving from the present authoritarian reality to the non-authoritarian ideal" is either absent (because rulership and hierarchy are accepted or espoused) or unrecognizable to those who read the *Daodejing, Zhuangzi,* and *Master Incapable* as political theory in the Western sense.[38] Most Daoists were convinced that anyone who tries to oppose the state or to fight the system will end up like the praying mantis in *Zhuangzi,* frantically waving its pincers in an attempt to stop the cartwheel that is about to crush it. The ways Daoist texts propose to redress the problem of rule are too different from Western political theory to be perceived as possible solutions.

Master Incapable has often been labeled a "nihilist," as he seems to be merely negating or attacking, and appears unable to suggest any remedies. It would be more accurate to say that in *Master Incapable*'s analysis, the human is a tragic species whose evolution from an animal that lived in a sort of chaotic harmony with the other animals into a social being driven by emotions, desires, and ambitions was caused by a profusion of the intellect. Intellect, like language, can be found everywhere, including among the other kinds of animals, but the abnormal growth of it in humankind has led to the creation of hierarchies and divisions between humans and animals, male and female, relatives and nonrelatives, rich and poor, noble and humble, and so on. According to Master Incapable, these hierarchies and divisions have been created in an unnatural

35 They include K. C. Hsiao in Republican China, and Sa Mengwu and Zhang Jinjian in Taiwan. See bibliography for details.
36 Exemplary of this trend is the work of John A. Rapp. For a review of Rapp 2012, see Pines 2014. Rapp's 1978 MA thesis is also on the relation between Daoism and anarchism.
37 See Ames 1983, 4.
38 See Ames 1983, 30–31.

fashion, using force (*qiang* 彊), and they have been perpetuated by the most intelligent of all human beings, "those whom one calls sages" (謂之聖人者), who succeeded in making mankind believe that their inventions—agriculture, architecture, hierarchy, moral codes, rituals, social conventions, and countless forms of punishment—possessed universal value and thus had every right to become immutable traditions.

In Master Incapable's vision, however, all these traditions and conventions are of no value at all, because they were created in a purely arbitrary fashion. They are the result of a process that in its most elementary form consists of what Master Incapable calls the forcible use of names (*qiangming* 彊名).[39] We may think that naming things is something rather innocent. What could possibly be wrong with naming a mountain "mountain"? Things become more problematic when humans start to use language to create differences or divisions between moral values such as "good" and "evil," "orthodox" and "unorthodox," and at the same time implement ways to promote "good" and "orthodox," and to punish "evil" and "unorthodox." To Master Incapable, naming things carries within itself the origin of the extreme violence to which he was witness in his day. By naming someone in the empire "ruler" and all the others "subjects," whereby the ruler is allowed to treat the masses as serfs, but the masses are not allowed to stand up to their ruler, one does not merely create a hierarchy, one also sows the seeds of jealousy, feelings of honor and dishonor, cravings and desires, competition and strife, or what Master Incapable calls the "quarrelsome mind." Neither the Confucian moral code nor the excessive use of laws, regulations, corporal punishment, or punitive expeditions is able to curb the long decline into utter misery and internecine warfare.

Another reason why the forcible use of names is without any value is that anyone can do it. This point is made most powerfully in the anecdote about Master Incapable and the madman in Book III ("Records of Things Witnessed" III), but it is also central to the longest and probably most acerbic among the recreations of historical episodes in Book II, about the hermit Yan Guang and the first Eastern Han emperor (see pp. 97 and 65).

As has already been hinted, Book II is a major statement on reclusion in a time when reclusion among literati was a widespread phenomenon. Indeed, the list of literati who temporarily or definitively eschewed

---

39 The very word *qiangming* implies a critique of the Confucian notion of "rectifying names" (*zhengming* 正名), according to which names are "rectified" when there is accordance between a name and what that name denotes, its reality, actuality, or substance. Without a rectification of names, Confucianism teaches, there can only be chaos.

government service in the second half of the ninth century is impressive. It includes the well-known poets Lu Guimeng 陸龜蒙 (d. ca. 881), Zhang Qiao 張喬 (ninth century), Fang Gan 方干 (ninth century), Du Xunhe 杜荀鶴 (846-904), and Sikong Tu 司空圖 (837-908). The reclusive behavior of *Master Incapable*'s author was anything but exceptional in an era when not only the court but also autonomous military governors and rebel leaders sought the services of famous writers for their staffs.[40] But the decision not to seek or accept government service, though partly inspired by a wish for self-preservation, did not always yield the result hoped for. When the poet Zhou Pu 周朴 (d. 878) travelled to the southeastern city of Fuzhou hoping to stay out of the claws of Huang Chao's rebel army, Huang Chao occupied Fuzhou and found Zhou Pu hiding as a recluse in a Buddhist monastery. When Huang Chao asked if he was willing to follow him, Zhou replied, "I don't even serve the emperor, why would I follow a bandit?"[41] at which the rebel leader had the poet beheaded on the spot. Likewise, when the great poet Sikong Tu was offered a ministership by Zhu Wen 朱溫 (852-912)—a former rebel who had been appointed Tang general and changed his name to Quanzhong 全忠, "Completely Loyal," (an example of Master Incapable's forceful renaming), and who then murdered Emperor Zhaozong in 904—he remained a recluse, because he was unwilling to accept high office from such a character. But when Zhu formally ended the Tang and had the last emperor, a fifteen-year-old boy, murdered, Sikong Tu starved himself to death. These historical examples can contextualize not only Master Incapable's reclusion, but the discussion of reclusion in *Master Incapable*, as well.

Master Incapable's discussions of reclusion are remarkably nuanced. Thus, Lü Wang, in the first chapter of Book II, is even allowed to give up his temporary reclusion and assist the future first Zhou king once he is convinced that the latter is not driven by private motivations or greed. The recreations of famous dialogues in Book II offer Master Incapable the chance to elaborate some of his major themes, among them mental

---

40 Thus, as the moral authority of the imperial court reached its nadir and the disintegration of the dynasty was well under way, the poet Li Shanfu 李山甫 (ninth century) served in the quasi autonomous province of Weibo 魏博; Gu Yun 顧雲 (?-894) served under Gao Pian 高駢 (821-887), who ruled the Huainan 淮南 region autonomously; Yin Wengui 殷文圭 (?-920) accepted a post from the founder of the small state of Wu 吳; Luo Yin, after many examination failures, took up service under Qian Liu 錢鏐 (852-932), future ruler of the state of Wu-Yue 吳越; Wei Zhuang 韋莊 (836-910) served Wang Jian 王建 (847-918), future emperor of the state of Shu 蜀; and Pi Rixiu 皮日休 (834–883 or later), according to tradition, even accepted the title of Hanlin Scholar 翰林學士 from the rebel leader Huang Chao in Chang'an.

41 To a Buddhist monk and a hermit, imperial authority carries little or no weight.

vacuity, the need to "obscure" oneself as a means to live out one's natural
lifespan, and warnings against the evils of civilization and the uncontrolled
growth of emotions. Several chapters such as "Discourses on Confucius,"
and "Discourse on Yan Ling" also contain sketches of a mystical union
with the Way. Another major theme of Book II, prominent in half of its
chapters, is that of fraudulence (*wang* 妄). It is the fraudulence not only of
rulers but even of hermits who pretend to act inspired by morality, while
in fact they are driven by desire and greed. It is the fraudulence of a Qu
Yuan, who is clearly delusional when he thinks that he can singlehandedly
make Chu into a state governed in a morally acceptable fashion; and it is
the fraudulence of an Emperor Guangwu, who tries to lure the recluse Yan
Guang into accepting an official post using official titles, ranks of nobility,
and dreams of power and glory as bait.

In Book III, the major themes are the opposition between consciously
directed, purposive, or motivated action (*youwei* 有為) and effortless or
non-intentional action, and the importance of "no-mind." The latter concept, in particular, is omnipresent in the third book, and Master Incapable
employs a wide variety of narratives and dialogues illustrating the benefits
of being "free of intentionality." In "Reply to Huayangzi's Question," no-
mind is central to the question of whether or not it is advisable to take up
government service. "Reply to Yuzhongzi's Question" is a very short dialogue suggesting that Master Incapable's bosom friend has spontaneously
come to the realization of no-mind. In the parable "Discourse on Fish," the
absence of intentionality is put in the context of fish changing into dragons
and of the natural mechanism behind it. And in the parable "Discourse on
the Poison Bird," a snake is eaten as punishment for possessing the "poison of intentionality." In both dialogues between Master Incapable and his
cousin Lu, no-mind is present, teamed up with naturalness, as a means to
avoid existential anxieties without becoming dependent on alcohol. In the
first of the "Records of Things Witnessed," Master Incapable explains how
a magician is able to keep himself from being burnt with "a body that has
been freed of the mind."

The book's final words—"Those who are enlightened turn their back
on custom"—remind us that Master Incapable's fundamental stance is
not primarily that of anarchism in the Western sense, but that of a radical
anti-conventionalism or anti-traditionalism. Master Incapable's reaction
to the gigantic existential challenges of his time is not despair, not even
some kind of "inner emigration," and certainly not a political program
for collective action aimed at ridding the world of rulers.[42] What Master Incapable proposes is a return to naturalness, simplicity, absence of

42 The quote is from Müller (2001, 118).

intentionality, and nonpurposive action. In that, he remains remarkably close to the message of the *Daodejing*, *Zhuangzi*, and *Liezi*. A "composite portrait" of *Master Incapable*'s consummate man, who in many cases is presented as a hermit or as someone who refuses to shine in an age of darkness, would look like the following. Not having forgotten that all creatures are the result of the spontaneous interaction of the life-forces of yin and yang, he does not create arbitrary divisions between himself and others, between humans and other animals. He makes effortless or nonpurposive action into the very foundation of his life. He is impervious to the fear of dying, knowing that the tangible components of his person have always been dead and therefore cannot die. He does not chase noble status or power, knowing they merely amount to possessing an abundance of material things, nor is he motivated by the desire for a good reputation, knowing that the body to which the reputation is attached is impermanent. He never grants emotions a leading role, knowing that it is appropriate for humans to be oblivious of one another in naturalness, just like it is appropriate for fish to forget one another in rivers and lakes. He can be soft and flexible like water, and thereby remain in touch with naturalness and keep his vital energies intact. Free of emotions and intentionality, he is an embodiment of heaven and earth. He cultivates himself without criticizing others, and he does not seek notoriety. Like Yan Guang, he is "submerged in the Great Void" (the total absence of distinctions) and he "feeds on the Great Harmony" (the harmoniously operating energies of heaven and earth). He immerses himself in Nullity and concentrates on the Permanent. In other words, he reaches mystical union with the Way, and he may choose any kind of action in everyday life, provided he is not guided by intentionality, profit, or desire.

Needless to say, choosing this path can only be the individual's own responsibility. In the words of the final chapter: "Nonpurposive action is our own choice, and cravings and desires are our own choice. Nonpurposive action leads to serenity, while cravings and desires lead to undertakings. Serenity leads to happiness, and undertakings lead to worrying." As Kristofer Schipper has written about early Daoist communities, individual responsibility was of the greatest significance, as there was no religious authority to enforce any rules or regulations: "The emphasis on the self, on the personal relationship to the Dao, implies, also with respect to the preservation of the natural environment, that each person is responsible for the Dao, each person embodies the Dao. The preservation of the natural order therefore depends absolutely on the preservation of this natural order and harmony within ourselves and not on some outside authority." Daoist precepts, he continues, "never speak of protests to the higher authorities, of political actions, revindications, demands for justice and peace, but only of respiration exercises, of inner harmony and individual peace. . . . To regulate the world, we have to cultivate ourselves, to tend our inner landscape."[43] The same ethic is on display in *Master Incapable*.

To my knowledge, no one has ever attempted to identify *Master Incapable*'s author, but that does not mean that such an attempt is pointless. An examination of the names of Master Incapable's contemporaries mentioned in the text offers a very limited (and ultimately inconclusive) possibility of identification. Master Incapable has conversations with a number of persons, some addressed collectively as his disciples (*tu* 徒), others known by their family or clan names, and still others with names that are undoubtedly fictitious. One name stands out because of its overt Daoist connotations, and that is Huayangzi 華陽子. Huayang indicates the eighth of the ten major Grotto-Heavens (*da dongtian* 大洞天), situated at Mount Gouqu 句曲山, better known as Mount Mao 茅山, in present-day Jiangsu Province. Historically, a number of well-known Daoists have used Huayang as part of their religious name.[44] In *Master Incapable*, Huayangzi is described not as a disciple or a family member but as a "friend of Master Incapable's body" or Master Incapable's "physical friend" (*xinghai zhi you* 形骸之友). This is a very curious, seemingly unprecedented expression. The modern editors Wang Ming and Zhang Songhui speculate that Huayangzi must be the opposite of an "intimate friend" (*xinyou* 心友), viewing the tangible body (*xinghai*) as the opposite of the mind (*xin* 心). Though this explanation has its validity, I would like to suggest a different line of thought: let us suppose that man is the best friend of his own body. In that case, could the author of *Master Incapable* not have created the double identity of the Incapable Master and his "physical friend" with the aim of having a conversation about one of the major topics of the book, namely, the question of whether or not to take up government service? If Master Incapable and the "friend of his body" were one and the same person, a possible candidate for the authorship of *Master Incapable* would be Zhang Bi 張賁 of Nanyang 南陽 (Henan province), who passed the Presented Scholar (*jinshi* 進士)

---

43 Schipper 2001, 91–92.
44 This includes the eminent scholar and compiler of the *Declarations of the Perfected* (*Zhen'gao* 真誥), Tao Hongjing 陶弘景 (456–536), known as Huayang yinju 華陽隱居 (Recluse of Huayang), and the Tang poet Gu Kuang 顧況 (c. 727–816), known as Huayang zhenyi 華陽真逸 (True Unconfined One of Huayang) or Huayang zhenyin 華陽真隱 (True Recluse of Huayang).

examination sometime between 847 and 860. Zhang Bi was later appointed Erudite in the Institute for the Extension of Literary Arts (*guangwen boshi* 廣文博士), in which capacity he would have been responsible for handling the training of students preparing to take the Presented Scholar exam.[45] He resurfaces in 870 as a Daoist living in reclusion on Mount Mao, a major Daoist center in Tang times that had excellent ties with the imperial court. To his own generation, Zhang Bi was known as Huayang shanren 華陽山人 (Mountain Man of Huayang) and Huayang daoshi 華陽道士 (Daoist Master of Huayang). What is left of his literary output all dates back to the year 870, when he exchanged poems with the great late Tang literati Lu Guimeng and Pi Rixiu, though admittedly these seventeen poems do not offer any clues about any possible relation between Zhang Bi, the recluse of Huayang, and Master Incapable or his "bodily friend" Huayangzi.

   Master Incapable brings different strands of thought into convergence. First and foremost there are echoes of the so-called "primitivist" chapters 9 and 10 from *Zhuangzi*. Chapter 9 of *Zhuangzi* states that in the era of perfect virtue humans lived together with the other animals, making no distinction whatsoever between "noble" and "humble." The chapter repeatedly points out the "fault of the sages," who destroyed the Way and its power or virtue, replacing it by humaneness and dutifulness, two of the cardinal Confucian virtues. In the tenth *Zhuangzi* chapter, the Way and knowledge are viewed as opposites, and the love of knowledge, accompanied by the lack of the Way, is considered the main cause of disorder in the empire.[46] In *Master Incapable* we also find echoes of the sixteenth *Zhuangzi* chapter, which deals with the destructive role of civilization and the irretrievable loss of man's inborn nature. However, whereas the radical nature of the *Zhuangzi*'s primitivist chapters is softened at points, implying that the Confucian hierarchization of society might be in accord with Daoist principles, *Master Incapable*'s virulently anti-Confucian stance is maintained throughout the work. Another main influence is that of the proto-anarchist Bao Jingyan.[47] Bao Jingyan was not the first one to suggest that in high antiquity there were no rulers, but before him no one had so forcefully defended the view that

---

45 The Tang dynasty was the first period during which the Chinese civil service examination system was used to recruit a part of the officials serving in the court bureaucracy, with the Presented Scholar the most prestigious of all examinations. Only one to two percent of the candidates—in some years there were up to two or three thousand—passed the examination.

46 On *Zhuangzi*'s primitivist chapters, see also Graham 1989, 306–311.

47 The depiction of Bao is that of his philosophical opponent Ge Hong in *The Master Who Embraces Simplicity*. On the link between Bao Jingyan and *Master Incapable*, see also Needham 1956, 436.

this alleged condition was superior to anything that came afterwards.[48] Bao Jingyan detested the idea, propagated by Confucian literati, that Heaven had given birth to the people and established rulers over them. Instead, according to Bao:

> The fact is that the strong oppressed the weak and the weak submitted to them; the cunning tricked the innocent and the innocent served them. It was because there was submission that the relation of lord and subject arose, and it was because there was servitude that the people, being powerless, could be kept under control. Thus, servitude and mastery result from the struggle between the strong and the weak and the contrast between the cunning and the innocent, and Blue Heaven has nothing whatsoever to do with it.[49]

In Bao Jingyan's sketch of the original state of mankind, when all living beings valued the Way and found contentment in self-fulfillment, humans led simple, free and easy lives of agricultural labor. In this utopian world, there was no competition or scheming and no form of hierarchy. There were no means of communication by water or land and thus no appropriation of each other's property and no attacks on other people. Man lived in total harmony with the other animals. Diseases did not spread, and thus everybody lived out a natural lifespan. People's hearts were pure; accumulation of riches was an unknown phenomenon. But somehow, decadence set in, the Way and its power fell into decay, and hierarchy was born. In his sketch of the disintegration of original simplicity, Master Incapable remains quite close to Bao Jingyan.[50]

The influence of *Liezi* is also strong, with its blurring of the boundaries between reality and illusion, its cosmogony, and its stress on mental emptiness as a basis for successful action. Minor influences include that of the rationalism and naturalism of Wang Chong 王充 (27–97) and even that of the legalist *Han Feizi* 韓非子. Master Incapable's mix of all these elements is more radical than the theories of his predecessors, and to my knowledge, no later thinker surpassed Master Incapable on this point. Fu Lo-shu has point-

---

48 We encounter such an opinion already in *Mr. Lü's Spring and Autumn Annals* (*Lüshi chunqiu* 呂氏春秋) completed in 239 BC.

49 See Balazs 1964, 243. Note that Balazs has only translated the first part of Bao Jingyan's opinions as found in *The Master Who Embraces Simplicity*. For a complete translation in French, see Levi 2004, 33–54.

50 Good introductions to Daoist utopianism are Bauer 1974, 61–84, 142–215; Hendrischke 2000; and Steavu 2014.

ed out the similarities between *Master Incapable* and the anti-autocratic philosophy of Deng Mu 鄧牧 (1247–1306), who in his turn served as the source for Huang Zongxi's 黃宗羲 (1610–1695) *Waiting for the Dawn: A Plan for the Prince* (*Mingyi daifang lu* 明夷待訪錄), but whether Deng Mu or Huang Zongxi were actually aware of *Master Incapable* is difficult to ascertain.[51]

As a work of literature, *Master Incapable* has hardly been studied. This is an unfortunate omission, as the text has its place in the development of the late Tang "ancient-style prose" movement. This movement was one aspect of a broader intellectual trend known as "return to antiquity" (*fugu* 復古). The period between the end of the Han dynasty and the early Tang had seen the flourishing of a literary prose style that eventually became known as "parallel prose" (*pianwen* 駢文 or *piantiwen* 駢體文), characterized by the use of pairs of lines of equal length with metrical identity and syntactical parallelism (familiar in poetry as well). Starting in the early Tang, certain prose writers reacted against this style, considering it artificial and frivolous. The Tang dynasty champions of that reaction, who advocated a return to a style that had its roots in the simpler language of the Confucian classics, were Han Yu 韓愈 (768–824) and Liu Zongyuan 柳宗元 (773–819). *Master Incapable* is not entirely free of parallel elements, but insofar as the term "ancient-style prose" encompasses all philosophical or moral "prose writings in which a straightforward, non-parallel style was employed to treat a single subject in an independent work or section of a work" and its language is rooted first and foremost in the prose writings of the pre-Qin philosophers, it fits the label.[52]

Reception

After having received a number of short notices in Song and Yuan dynasty bibliographies (see below), *Master Incapable* enjoyed a degree of popularity in Ming times. As we saw, the work was reprinted by Ming imperial princes, but it also attracted the attention of some Confucian literati. This is evident from Gui Youguang's 歸有光 (1507–1571) *Casket Collecting Various*

---

51 Fu 1965, 68, n. 1 and 72, n. 1.

52 See Nienhauser 1986, 494. One of the prose subgenres promoted by the early ancient-style prose proponents, such as Han Yu and Liu Zongyuan, was the "discourse" or "explanation" (*shuo* 說). In his comprehensive study of Late Tang and Five Dynasties prose literature, Lü Wuzhi 呂武志 inventoried a total of twenty "explanations" written by nine authors (see Lü Wuzhi 1989, 388–418). Lü does not mention *Master Incapable*, presumably because it is a Masters Text and therefore not primarily considered literary, but we could argue that to these twenty, Master Incapable adds another twelve: all the chapters in Book II, as well as two chapters in Book III.

Masters (*Zhuzi huihan* 諸子彙函), a late Ming collection of fragments of Masters Texts. The *Casket* contains only five *Master Incapable* chapters ("Discourse on King Wen," "Discourse on Song Yu," "Discourse on the Hermits of Shang," "Discourse on Yan Ling" and "Discourse on the Poison Bird"), but these chapters are accompanied by commentaries written by a number of rather well-known Ming-dynasty literati, among them Zou Zhi 鄒智 (1466–1491), Cai Qing 蔡清 (1453–1508), Yang Shen 楊慎 (1488–1559) and Wang Shizhen 王世貞 (1526–1590). However, the oldest piece of commentary on *Master Incapable* in the *Casket* goes back (if authentic) to the eleventh century. It is a short but not unsympathetic remark on the text by the Neo-Confucian philosopher Cheng Hao 程顥 (1032–1085), who summarizes *Master Incapable* as being essentially interested in the elucidation of the principle of naturalness and exploring the boundaries of human nature and of the heavenly-ordained lifespan. In fact, Cheng Hao is merely repeating a fragment of *Master Incapable*'s preface, for he continues with the following words: "In naturalness one is without undertaking; human nature and the heavenly-ordained lifespan are free of desire." However, in the final sentence, there is a marked difference from the text of the preface, because instead of stating that Master Incapable was someone who neglected (*lüe* 略) the "doctrine of the rites" (i.e., Confucianism) and kept worldly matters at a distance, Cheng Hao states that Master Incapable revered (*chong* 崇) Confucianism, which seems somewhat surprising, to say the least.

After the establishment of the People's Republic of China, scholars began to pay attention to *Master Incapable*, with Bu Jinzhi's 步近智 1980 article on progressive thought in the Late Tang and Five Dynasties period, and of course the 1981 publication of the first modern critical edition of *Master Incapable*, edited by Wang Ming 王明. Wang Ming's edition came with a well-researched preface titled "Master Incapable's Philosophical Thought" (无能子的哲學思想). As the article's subtitle "An Outstanding Work Influenced by the Great Peasant Uprisings of the End of the Tang" (唐末農民大起義影響下一部特出的著作) makes clear, the interest in *Master Incapable* was sparked by the attention to popular uprisings during the 1970s in the PRC.[53]

---

53 A good late-1970s introduction to this topic is Hu Rulei 1979. Fan Jiliu (1983) offers a highly detailed account of Huang Chao's rebellion, completed in 1980. The interest in peasant uprisings was tightly linked to the political climate of the Cultural Revolution (1966–1969, but in fact lasting until Mao Zedong's death in 1976). The stated aim of the Cultural Revolution was to free Chinese communism from capitalism and from bourgeois and traditionalist elements. As poor farmers, along with workers and soldiers, were considered most worthy of respect in Maoist thought, it was only logical that historians would look for what could be seen as proto-communist uprisings within the lower societal classes.

Chinese scholarly articles from the 1980s remained obsessed with whether the text was "materialistic," and therefore good, or "idealistic," and therefore bad. Wang Ming's rather mitigated judgment, that *Master Incapable* presented a mix of naïve materialism and a naturalist viewpoint with, alas, a strong presence of metaphysical characteristics, was challenged by Zhu Yueli 朱越利 in 1983 and Li Xi 李曦 in 1985, with the typical plethora of quasi-insults popular in those days.[54] The scholarly value of such articles or book chapters is negligible, but the influence they exerted, in particular concerning Buddhist influence, is not to be underestimated.[55]

Master Incapable receives a more sympathetic treatment in Li Junheng's 李俊恒 1987 article, which praises Master Incapable for his stance against superstition and for his opposition to the theory of the heavenly mandate, arguing that the book gives voice to the oppressed peasant population.[56] Articles from the 1990s worth mentioning include Quan Genxian's 全根先 1991 inquiry into the different philosophical sources that contributed to the formation of Master Incapable's system of thought and Zhao Jun's 趙俊 1999 claim that Master Incapable was one of "three heroes" of Late-Tang thought.[57] Since 2000, scholarly attitudes towards *Master Incapable* have been predominantly positive and reflect new fashions and fields of interest, such as the ecological dimension of the text, and new approaches to the text's philosophical influences.[58]

The single most influential publication on *Master Incapable* was the 1936 article "Anarchism in Chinese Political Thought" by K. C. Hsiao (Xiao Gongquan 蕭公權, 1897–1981), a liberal socialist Chinese historian and political scientist who first came to the United States in 1920 and taught at Yenching and Tsinghua Universities after returning temporarily to China. Before that, Alfred Forke's pioneering 1934 study, *Geschichte der mittelalterlichen chinesischen Philosophie* [History of Medieval Chinese Philosophy] is among the very first Western sinological works to pay attention to *Master Incapable*, and recognizes that the text expresses highly original views con-

---

54 Li Xi 1985, 391–426. In his article, Zhu even suggests that Master Incapable might have gone insane with despair.
55 Rapp 2012.
56 Li Junheng 1987.
57 Quan Genxian 1991; Zhao Jun 1999. Pi Rixiu and Luo Yin were the other two.
58 For ecological dimensions, see Li Guangfu 2005. On philosophical influences, see Sun Gongjin 2010 and Tan Min 2011. Jiang Yiwei 2018 presents a synthesis of Master Incapable's thought, but adds little new insight.

cerning the relationship between body and mind, between life and death, and between man and the other animals.[59]

Despite Hsiao's claim that Master Incapable "made by far the most eloquent statement on Chinese anarchism," he considers Master Incapable's anarchism to be "a pure negation, a denunciation of the state without any suggestion as to what is to be done or what shall take the place of the state."[60] The influence of such a view extends to Gert Naundorf's "Zum anarchischen Gedanken in China" [On Anarchist Thought in China] in which he presents *Master Incapable* as a late flowering of the Daoist anarchist thought found in *Zhuangzi* and Bao Jingyan. It also extends to Peter Zarrow, who says that Master Incompetent "traced the devolution of society from ancient community to agriculture and selfishness, kings, bureaucracy, and the institution of morality, laws, wars, and constant suffering. Wunengzi was closer to being a total cynic than a constructive social thinker."[61] Like Hsiao, Zarrow seems not to have noticed the solutions Master Incapable proposes with an eye to finding a way out of mankind's predicament: a radical break with all conventions and traditions, a return to naturalness and to the "absence of mind." Hence his conclusion regarding Master Incapable's perceived cynicism. Gotelind Müller's thoroughly researched *China, Kropotkin und der Anarchismus* [China, Kropotkin, and Anarchism], though, recognizes the importance in Master Incapable's thought of the arbitrary nature of name giving and of the separation between mankind and the animal world. In Müller's view, the dominant mood in *Master Incapable* is close to despair, just as it is in the case of Bao Jingyan, and as John A. Rapp would also do, she asks herself whether Master Incapable's stance might not be best described as nihilism.[62]

To date, the most insightful treatment of *Master Incapable* in a Western language is Dominic Steavu's 2014 article "Cosmogony and the Origin of Inequality: A Utopian Perspective from Taoist Sources." Looking beyond the narrow political dimension, Steavu identifies aspects of Master Incapable's analysis such as the return to naturalness and effortless action, as well

---

59 Forke 1964, 326–332. Forke also quotes the opening lines of *Master Incapable* describing the formation of the universe and its inhabitants in his book *The World-Conception of the Chinese* (Forke 1925, 56–57). Before that, *Master Incapable* had received short bibliographic notices in an 1878 contribution by August Pfizmaier, quoted in Naundorf 1972, 29–30 and in Wieger 1911, nr. 1016.

60 Hsiao 1936, 259, 260. Hsiao devoted a chapter to *Master Incapable* in his magnum opus (1945), and his example was followed by other authors of extensive histories of Chinese political thought, such as the Taiwanese writers Sa Mengwu 1969 and Zhang Jinjian 1989.

61 Zarrow 1990, 10. One year later, in Dirlik 1991, *Master Incapable* is not mentioned.

62 Müller 2001, 116–118.

as the return to what Steavu describes as "a realisation of the tenets of inner nature and vital force (*xingming* 性命) without desiring it (*wuyu* 無欲)."[63]

A Note on the text

Is the *Master Incapable* text we possess now the full text? I argue yes, despite the fact that the editio princeps marks a number of chapters as missing. The editio princeps of *Master Incapable* is that of the *Daoist Canon of the Zhengtong Reign* (*Zhengtong daozang* 正統道藏), a Ming-dynasty work completed during the Zhengtong reign period (1439–1449). The *Daoist Canon* edition is the only complete version of *Master Incapable*, with the three books preceded by the preface and a table of contents. Editions such as the *Complete Library of the Four Repositories*, the *One Hundred Masters Texts* (*Zishu baijia* 子書百家), the *Complete Writings of the Hundred Masters* (*Baizi quanshu* 白子全書) and the *Complete Collection of Books from Various Collectanea* (*Congshu jicheng* 叢書集成), all of which copy the late Ming *The Masters Collocated* (*Zihui* 字彙) edition, all omit the table of contents.

Master Incapable is mentioned in a number of Song-dynasty catalogs, among them the *General Catalog of the Academy for the Veneration of Literature* (*Chongwen zongmu* 崇文總目, compiled 1042), the bibliographic chapter on Daoist texts in the *New History of the Tang* (*Xin Tang shu* 新唐書, compiled 1060), the *Later Monograph on Books Read in the Commandery Studio* (*Junzhai dushu houzhi* 郡齋讀書後志, 1250), and the *Explanatory Notes on Cataloged Books in the Studio of Straightforwardness* (*Zhizhai shulu jieti* 直齋書錄解題, mid-1200s).[64] The very short notices devoted to *Master Incapable* in these catalogs repeat information from the preface: the book was written during the Guangqi reign period by someone who went into hiding among the populace without revealing his identity. Concerning the exact volume of the text, the *Later Monograph on Books Read in the Commandery Studio* states that it amounts to thirty chapters (*pian* 篇), and this information is copied in Ma Duanlin's 馬端臨 (1254?–1323?) Yuan dynasty *Comprehensive Examination of Literary Documents* (*Wenxian tongkao* 文獻通考) as well as in the *Essentials of the General Catalog of the Complete Library of the Four Repositories* (*Siku quanshu zongmu tiyao* 四庫全書總目提要). The compilers of the latter work drew attention to the fact that the present text consists of thirty-four instead of thirty chapters. They furthermore stated that in the original table of contents (not copied into the *Complete Library of the Four Repositories*), a total of eight chapters were marked as

---

63 Steavu 2014, 316.
64 See Loon 1984, 143.

"missing": chapter 6 in Book I, chapter 5 in Book II, and no less than six chapters (7, 9, 10, 12, 13, and 14) in Book III. This led the compilers of the *Complete Library of the Four Repositories* to speculate on the possibility that the original *Master Incapable* contained not thirty-four but forty-two chapters, and to wonder whether the preface, which mentions a total of thirty-four chapters, had been tampered with so as to make it correspond with the chapter count of the received text.

In fact, the number of chapters marked as missing in the original table of contents is even higher than the one mentioned in the *Essentials of the General Catalog of the Complete Library of the Four Repositories*, as it also includes chapters 8, 9, and 10 in Book I. Following the logic of the *Complete Library of the Four Repositories*, the original *Master Incapable* would then have contained forty-five chapters. There is, however, no reason to assume that the present text is not the complete *Master Incapable*, and this is suggested by the pattern of chapter titles and chapters marked as missing. Thus, the fifth chapter in Book I is said in the table of contents to consist of two pieces, and it is followed by a sixth chapter marked as missing. The seventh chapter in the same book is said to consist of four pieces, and it is followed by an eighth, ninth, and tenth chapter marked as missing. In Book II, the two-part chapter 4 is followed by a "missing" fifth chapter. The same pattern occurs in the third book, where the sixth chapter, said to consist of two pieces, is followed by a "missing" seventh chapter; the eighth chapter, said to consist of three pieces, is followed by two "missing" chapters, and the eleventh chapter, said to consist of four pieces, is followed by chapters 12, 13, and 14 marked as missing. What this suggests is that the maker of the table of contents, whoever he was, focused on chapter headings instead of on the actual number of chapters or pieces. Thus, for example, he correctly noted that the fourth chapter of Book II, titled "Discourses on Confucius," consists of two pieces (one containing a dialogue between Confucius and his disciple Zilu, and the other involving Confucius and his disciples Yuan Xian and Zigong), but because the second piece lacked a separate title, he concluded that the next chapter must have disappeared.[65]

The number given of thirty chapters in the *Later Monograph on Books Read in the Commandery Studio,* although probably a scribal error, has led some contemporary scholars, among them Zhu Yueli, to surmise that the final four chapters of *Master Incapable*, titled "Consolidating the Foundation" (*guben* 固本), were later additions, probably dating from the Ming

65 Jiang An follows the same line of reasoning and concludes that the present Master Incapable is the complete text. See Jiang An 1983, 345.

dynasty.[66] Zhu Yueli argues that the final four chapters do not fit well in Book III, that they are clumsily written, and that they could not be added to Book I, because they would read as repetitions of content already treated there. In my view, there is no factual basis supporting Zhu's assumption. The final four chapters do exactly what is promised in their title: they consolidate the foundation, namely nonpurposive action, as explained in the second chapter of Book I. *Master Incapable*'s final advice, to turn one's back on custom, is announced in the third section of the chapter "Records of Things Witnessed," where Master Incapable is lectured by a madman on the arbitrary nature of language. Moreover, we even have a late-Ming source that implicitly authenticates *Master Incapable*'s final four chapters as dating to the Tang. This source, which I have not found mentioned in any discussion of *Master Incapable*, is Chen Yumou's 陳禹謀 *A Treatise in Pairs* (*Pian zhi* 駢志), an encyclopedia (*leishu* 類書) from the Wanli era (1573–1620). The twentieth and last chapter of this work quotes the second of the final four *Master Incapable* chapters, on coffin makers and doctors being compelled by profit. In the preface to *A Treatise in Pairs*, dated 1606, Chen Yumou states that his sources are predominantly historical and philosophical, and that he very seldom has to resort to sources later than the Sui and Tang dynasties. The evidence is not conclusive, but it implies that Chen perceived the concluding *Master Incapable* chapters as authentic Tang material.

Translations

The first full translation of *Master Incapable* was made by Gert Naundorf into German, as part of his unpublished PhD thesis "Aspekte des anarchischen Gedankens in China. Darstellung der Lehre und Übersetzung des Textes Wu Neng Tzu" [Aspects of Anarchist Thought in China: Presentation of the Teaching and Translation of the Text *Wunengzi*]. The first English-language translation of the entire text dates from 1997 and was again part of an unpublished work (which I have not been able to consult), Nathan Woolley's "*Wunengzi* and the Early *Zhuangzi* Commentaries," a BA honors thesis. The first published translation was my Dutch-language *Nietskunner. Het taoïsme en de bevrijding van de geest* [Wunengzi: Daoism and the Liberation of the Mind], which dates from 2011 and is a thoroughly revised version of an unpublished translation made in 1986, while I studied at Fudan University with Professor Wang Guo'an 王國安. In 2012, an English-language rendition of *Master Incapable* was published as part of the appendices to John A.

---

66 Zhu Yueli 1983, 107.

Rapp's *Daoism and Anarchism*, but errors and imprecisions are frequent, the transcription of Chinese names is sloppy, and the annotation is feeble.

For the present translation, I have stayed as close as possible to the editio princeps, that of the Ming-dynasty Daoist canon. I follow many of the emendations found in Wang Ming's 1981 edition of the text, which takes into consideration the variants proposed by the late Ming *The Masters Collocated* edition, except where I deem it wiser to stick with the *Daoist Canon* readings. I have not translated the table of contents as in the *Daoist Canon*, and I make no mention of any "missing" chapters, as this only adds an unnecessary measure of confusion.

Master Incapable

无能子
无能子序

　　无能子，余忘形友也。少博學寡欲，長於窮理盡性，以至於命。黃巢亂，避地流轉，不常所處，凍餒淡如也。

　　光啟三年，天子在襃，四方猶兵。无能子寓於左輔景氏民舍，自晦也。民舍之陋，雜處其間，循循如也。晝好臥不寐，臥則筆札一二紙，興則懷之，而不余示。自仲春壬申至季春己亥，盈數十紙，卷而囊之，似有所著者。余竊得之，多紀所傳所見，或嘗與昆弟朋友問答之言。其旨歸於明自然之理，極性命之端。自然無作，性命無欲，

1　A friend with whom one has forgotten all outer forms of polite conduct.
2　Advised in *Daodejing* 19.
3　In other words, Master Incapable is described as being equal to the sages of antiquity who were responsible for creating the *Classic of Changes*. 窮理盡性以至於命 is a quote from the opening paragraph of the "Discussion of the trigrams" (*shuogua* 說卦), one of the commentaries to the *Classic of Changes*.

Preface

Master Incapable is an intimate friend of mine.[1] At a young age he was already widely learned and limited in his desires.[2] He excelled in the most thorough study of the cosmic order and of fundamental nature, and thus arrived at an understanding of the heavenly-ordained lifespan.[3] During the Huang Chao Rebellion, he fled and drifted, never staying long in one place and seemingly indifferent to cold and hunger.

In the third year of the Guangqi reign period, the Son of Heaven was in Bao, and in the four directions there was still warfare. Master Incapable lodged in the commoner's house of the Jing family in Zuofu, and concealed himself there.[4] Crude though his commonfolk lodgings were, he shared in the life there and conformed to it.

During the daytime, he liked to lie in bed without sleeping. Lying there, he would fill a few sheets of paper with writing. When he got up, he would keep them close to his chest without showing them to me. Between the *renshen* day of the second spring month and the *jihai* day of the final spring month, he filled a few dozen sheets of paper, which he rolled up and put in a bag.[5] It seemed as though he had written a book.

I secretly obtained this book. For the most part, it consists of records of things transmitted or witnessed, and in some cases, conversations he once had with brothers and friends. Its purport is essentially to illuminate the principle of naturalness and explore the boundaries of human nature and the heavenly-ordained lifespan. In naturalness one is without undertaking; human nature and the heavenly-ordained lifespan are free

---

4 The year is 887. Bao is short for Baocheng 褒城, the town southwest of Chang'an where Emperor Xizong resided after his flight from the capital in 886. Zuofu, the "Adjunct Region to the Left," also known as Zuo Pingyi 左馮翊, was an old administrative region east of Chang'an. The family name Jing 景 ("luminescent") was rather uncommon during the Tang. Interestingly, the Nestorian Church in China, present in Chang'an since the seventh century, was known as Da Qin Jingjiao 大秦景教 or "luminescent teachings from Great Qin." Wang Ming has suggested that the Qin mentioned in *Master Incapable*'s Book III is short for Da Qin 大秦, the Chinese name for the idealized Roman Empire, the Near East, or perhaps India (Wang Ming 1981, 43, n. 1; see also the annotation to "Records of Things Witnessed" I).

5 In traditional China, days received names combining a first character from a series of ten so-called "heavenly stems" and a second one from a series of twelve so-called "earthly branches."

是以略禮教而外世務焉。知之者不待喻而信，不知者能無罪
乎！余因析為品目，凡三十四篇，編上中下三卷，自與知之
者共之爾。余蓋具審无能子行止中藏，故不述其姓名游宦
焉。

---

6 The doctrine of the rites (*lijiao* 禮教) refers to Confucianism.
7 The wording of the latter part of this sentence (*neng wu zui hu* 能無罪乎) is ambiguous.
   Without any indication of either subject or object, it is impossible to determine who
   blames whom. Another possible translation is: Would those who do not understand be
   able not to blame [Master Incapable]?

of desire. Therefore Master Incapable neglects the doctrine of the rites and keeps worldly matters at a distance.[6] Those who understand this will put their faith in it without having to rely on further explanations. As to those who do not understand, could they be without blame?[7]

I have divided the text and ordered it thematically. A total of thirty-four chapters has been compiled into three books. I share the text with others who understand it.[8] I have closely examined both Master Incapable's actions and his deepest thoughts and feelings. Therefore, I make no mention of his name or his official career.[9]

8 Alternative translation: I share the text with others who know him [Master Incapable].
9 The term *youhuan* 游宦 suggests that Master Incapable was either an itinerant scholar or a government official on assignment away from the capital.

BOOK I
无能子卷上

聖過

天地未分，混沌一炁。一炁充溢，分為二儀。有清濁焉，有
輕重焉。輕清者上，為陽為天；重濁者下，為陰為地矣。天
則剛健而動，地則柔順而靜，炁之自然也。天地既位，陰陽
炁交，於是裸蟲、鱗蟲、毛蟲、羽蟲、甲蟲生焉。人者，裸
蟲也；與夫鱗毛羽甲蟲俱焉，同生天地，交炁而已，無所異
也。

　　或謂有所異者，豈非乎人自謂異於鱗羽毛甲諸蟲者？豈
非乎能用智慮耶，言語耶？夫自鳥獸迨乎蠢蠕，皆好生避
死，營其巢穴，謀其飲啄，生育乳養其類而護之；與人之好
生避死，營其宮室，謀其衣食，生育乳養其男女而私之，無
所異也。何可謂之無智慮耶？夫自鳥獸迨乎蠢蠕者，號鳴嘷
噪，皆有其音，安知其族類之中非語言耶？人以不喻其音，
而謂其不能言。又安知乎鳥獸不喻人言，亦謂人不能語言
耶？

10 In the choice of words for the title we can see the influence of *Zhuangzi* 9.
11 Master Incapable's language reflects that of the commentaries to the *Classic of Changes*,
    especially the "Commentary on the Appended Phrases" (*Xici zhuan* 繫辭傳). Needham
    describes Master Incapable's view as typical for the centrifugal cosmogony as found in
    Liezi, *Huainanzi* 淮南子, and the work of the Han dynasty skeptical thinker Wang Chong.
    See Needham 1956, 373.

The Fault of the Sages

Before heaven and earth separated, there was the undivided life-force of Chaos.[10][i] The undivided life-force overflowed and separated into the two Principles. There were the pure and the turbid, as well as the light and the heavy. The light and pure rose up, becoming yang and heaven; the heavy and turbid descended, becoming yin and the earth. Heaven, being firm and sturdy, was mobile; while earth, being soft and compliant, was immobile.[11] That was the spontaneous nature of the life-force.[12] Once heaven and earth had occupied their positions, the life-forces of yin and yang began to interact. Thereupon, the naked creatures, the scaly creatures, the hairy creatures, the feathered creatures, and the shelled creatures came into existence. Humans are the naked creatures. They live together with the scaly, hairy, feathered, and shelled creatures.[ii] Along with them, they are born from the interacting life-forces of heaven and earth, and there is nothing that sets them apart from the others.

Now, there are those who claim that there is something which sets them apart. Is it not true that humans call themselves different from the scaly, hairy, feathered, and shelled creatures? Are humans not able to make use of intellect and language? But however you look at it, from the birds and the beasts right down to the tiniest of the wriggling worms, all creatures love life and avoid death. They all build their nests and burrows, and seek out drink and food. They all raise and nurture their own kind and protect them. In no way do they differ from humans, who love life and avoid death, who build houses and habitations, who seek out clothing and food, who raise and nurture sons and daughters, and consider them theirs. How can it be claimed that the other creatures lack intellect?[13] From the birds and the beasts right down to the tiniest of wriggling worms, all creatures have their own sounds, whether it be shouts, bird song, twittering, or buzzing. How do you know that there is no language among them? It is only because humans do not understand these sounds that they claim that animals cannot speak. Furthermore, how do we know that the birds and the beasts, not understanding the language of humans, do not similarly claim mankind to be incapable of

---

12 "Spontaneous nature" here is *ziran* 自然, "what-is-so-of-itself."
13 A similar argument is put forward in the second chapter of *Liezi*. See Graham 1960, 54; Yang Bojun 1985, 84.

則其號鳴啅噪之音必語言爾。又何可謂之不能語言耶？智慮語言，人與蟲一也，所以異者形質爾。夫鱗毛羽甲中，形質亦有不同者，豈特止與人不同耶？人之中，形質亦有同而異者、異而同者，豈特止與四蟲之形質異也？

嗟乎！天與地，陰陽氣中之巨物爾。裸鱗羽毛甲五靈，因巨物合和之炁，又物於巨物之內，亦猶江海之含魚鼈，山陵之包草木爾。

所以太古時，裸蟲與鱗毛羽甲雜處，雌雄牝牡，自然相合，無男女夫婦之別，父子兄弟之序。夏巢冬穴，無宮室之制。茹毛飲血，無百穀之食。生自馳，死自仆，無奪害之心，無瘞藏之事。任其自然，遂其天真，無所司牧，濛濛淳淳，其理也居且久矣。

無何，裸蟲中繁其智慮者，其名曰人，以法限鱗毛羽甲諸蟲。又相教播種以食百穀，於是有耒耜之用。構木合土

---

14 The "five kinds of spiritually potent beings" (*wuling* 五靈) usually denotes the five aus-
picious animals: unicorn, phoenix, dragon, turtle, and white tiger.

speech? The shouting, singing, twittering, or buzzing sounds they make must therefore be considered language! How could one claim them incapable of speech? In the possession of both intellect and language, humans and the other creatures are one. The differences are only in the outward appearance. Now, differences in outward appearance also exist among the scaly, hairy, feathered, and shelled creatures. Why then solely insist on their being different from humans? Humans are also different one from another despite similarities in outward appearance, or alike in spite of their differences in outward appearance. Why solely insist on outward differences with regard to the other four kinds of creatures?

Heaven and earth are gigantic entities amidst the life-forces of yin and yang. In their turn, the five kinds of spiritually potent beings—to wit, the naked, scaly, hairy, feathered, and shelled creatures—are entities within the gigantic entities, as a result of the harmoniously conjoined life-forces of these gigantic entities.[14] Compare it to the way rivers and seas enclose fish and turtles, or the way mountains and hills contain grasses and trees.

Thus, in earliest antiquity, the naked creatures dwelled together with the scaly, hairy, feathered, and shelled creatures in a disorganized fashion.[15] Females and males united spontaneously, without any distinction between man and woman, or husband and spouse, and without any hierarchy between father and son, or older and younger brother. In summertime they lived in nests, in wintertime in burrows, and there was no construction of habitations. They devoured other creatures unskinned and drank their blood, and did not eat the hundred grains. After birth, they instinctively started to run. At the moment of death, they instinctively fell to the ground. No one gave a thought to stealing or murdering, and burials were an unknown custom. They depended on their spontaneous nature and followed their natural authenticity; they were neither controlled nor governed. Simplicity and purity were the ordering principles, and this situation lasted for a long time.[iii]

Later, among the naked creatures there were some whose intellect grew to be more rampant.[16] They were called humans. By means of laws they restricted the scaly, hairy, feathered, and shelled creatures. They also taught each other how to sow and plant in order to eat the hundred grains, and thereupon, plows began to be used. They joined pieces of

15 In the context of human relations, which are of crucial importance in Confucianism, za 雜 almost always has a pejorative connotation, carrying with it the meaning of "impure" or "bastardization."

16 That this profusion is no blessing is suggested by the fact that fan 繁 also has the connotation of "troublesomely many" or "vexatious."

以建宮室，於是有斤斧之功。設婚嫁以析雌雄牝牡，於是有
夫婦之別，父子兄弟之序。為棺槨衣衾以瘞藏其死，於是有
喪葬之儀。結罝罘綱羅以取鱗毛羽甲諸蟲，於是有刀俎之
味。濛淳以之散，情意以之作。然猶自強自弱，無所制焉。
繁其智慮者，又於其中擇一以統眾，名一為君，名眾為臣。
一可役眾，眾不得淩一。於是有君臣之分，尊卑之節，尊者
隆，眾者同。

　　降及後世，又設爵祿以升降其眾，於是有貴賤之等用其
物，貧富之差得其欲，乃謂繁智慮者為聖人。既而賤慕貴，
貧慕富，而人之爭心生焉。謂之聖人者憂之，相與謀曰，彼
始濛濛淳淳，孰謂之人？吾彊名之曰人。人蟲乃分。彼始無
卑無尊，孰謂之君臣？吾彊建之，乃君乃臣。彼始無取無
欲，何謂爵祿？吾彊品之，乃榮乃辱。今則醨真淳、厚嗜欲
而包爭心矣。爭則奪，奪則亂，將如之何？智慮愈繁者曰，
吾有術焉，於是立仁義忠信之教、

17 This is the first time that Master Incapable uses the crucial concept of *qiangming* 彊名.
    The origin is in verse 25 of the *Daodejing*, where it is said in an attempt to describe the
    Way: "Forced to name it, I would say: great" 吾強為之名曰大. In the *Daodejing*, forcible
    naming does not yet have the negative overtones it will acquire in *Master Incapable*.

wood together and mixed mud so as to build habitations, and thereupon, mattocks and axes were put to work. They established marriage,
thereby separating women from men, and consequently there was a
distinction between husband and wife, and a ranking of father and son,
and older and younger brother. Inner and outer coffins, clothing, and
shrouds were made to bury the dead, and thereupon the ritual obser-
vances connected with burial came into being. They knotted snares and
nets so as to capture the scaly, hairy, feathered, and shelled creatures,
and thereupon a taste for the knife and sacrificial meat-tray appeared.
Because of this, simplicity and purity faded, and emotions and intentions arose. However, creatures were still spontaneously strong or weak,
without anything being controlled. Those whose intellect had grown
most profusely selected one of their own to govern the masses. They
named this individual the "ruler" and they named the masses "subjects."
This individual was allowed to treat the masses as serfs, while the masses
were not allowed to confront the individual.[iv] Thereupon there was
the division between ruler and subject, and the segmentation between
venerable and lowly. The venerable one is prominent, while the masses
are all identical.

In the descent to later generations, ranks of nobility and official salaries were implemented to promote or demote the masses. Thereupon
one used things according to the classification of noble and humble,
and one satisfied one's desires according to the difference between
poor and rich. Consequently, those whose intellect had increased most
profusely were called "sages." Shortly after that, the humble became
jealous of the noble, and the poor became jealous of the rich, and so
the quarrelsome human mind arose. Those called sages were concerned
by this and consulted with one another: "At first, these creatures were
simple and pure. Who called them 'humans'? We forcibly named them
'humans,' whereupon they were separated from the other creatures.[17]
At first, among these creatures no one was humble or venerable. Who
called them 'ruler' or 'subject'? We forcibly established this, and since
then we have had rulers and subjects.[v] At first, capturing and desiring
were unknown to these creatures. Where did the ranks of nobility and
official salaries come from? We forced classifications upon them, and
since then there is honor and disgrace. The result is that now we have
watered down authenticity and purity, and intensified cravings and
desires, so that they harbor quarrelsome minds. The quarrelsome will
take by force, and taking by force leads to disorder. What should we
do?" Those whose intellect had grown even more profusely said: "We
have techniques for that." Whereupon they established the teachings
of humaneness, dutifulness, wholeheartedness, and trustworthiness,

禮樂之章以拘之。君苦其臣曰苛，臣侵其君曰叛，父不愛子
曰不慈，子不尊父曰不孝，兄弟不相順為不友不悌，夫婦不
相一為不貞不和。為之者為非，不為之者為是。是則榮，非
則辱，於是樂是恥非之心生焉，而爭心抑焉。

　　降及後代，嗜欲愈熾，於是背仁義忠信、踰禮樂而爭
焉。謂之聖人者悔之，不得已乃設刑法與兵以制之，小則刑
之，大則兵之。於是縲紲桎梏鞭笞流竄之罪充於國，戈鋋弓
矢之伐充於天下，覆家亡國之禍，綿綿不絕，生民困貧夭折
之苦，漫漫不止。

　　嗟乎！自然而蟲之，不自然而人之。彊立宮室飲食以誘
其欲，彊分貴賤尊卑以激其爭，彊為仁義禮樂以傾其真，彊
行刑法征伐以殘其生，俾逐其末而忘其本，紛其情而伐其
命，迷迷相死，古今不復，謂之聖人者之過也。

18　In this sentence we find the essence of the Confucian value system: *ren* 仁, *yi* 義, *zhong*
　　忠, *xin* 信, *li* 禮, and *yue* 樂. I alternately translate *li* as "ritual" and "etiquette."

and standards for ritual and music, in order to restrain them.[18] A ruler causing suffering to his subjects is called "pitiless," and subjects attacking their ruler are called "rebels." A father who is not fond of his son is called "unkind," and a son who does not respect his father is called "lacking in filial devotion." Older and younger brothers who do not get along are called "lacking in friendship and brotherly love," and a husband and wife without unity are called "lacking in chastity and harmony." Those who behave like this are considered wrong, and those who do not behave like this are considered right. If one is right, one is honored, and if one is wrong, one is dishonored. This, then, gave rise to a mentality of pleasure in what is right and shame in what is wrong. And so the quarrelsome mind was suppressed.

In the descent to later times, cravings and desires blazed up ever higher, whereupon humans turned their back on humaneness, dutifulness, wholeheartedness, and trustworthiness, transgressed ritual and music, and began to fight. Those called sages regretted this and saw no other option but to establish laws of corporal punishment and armaments as a means of control. For minor crimes, there was corporal punishment, and for major crimes, weapons were used. Thereupon the states were filled with crimes punished by restraining ropes, shackles and manacles, whips and bamboo canes, and banishment and exile, and the empire was filled with punitive expeditions and the use of swords, spears, bows, and arrows.[vi] Families were disrupted and states overthrown continuously. The people lived in dire straits and poverty, and the misery of premature deaths extended endlessly.

Alas! Naturalness is now for animals, and an absence of naturalness is for humans. They forcibly impose habitations, drink, and food, which leads to desire. They forcibly divide noble and humble, venerable and lowly, provoking struggles between humans.[vii] They forcibly implement humaneness, dutifulness, rituals, and music, overturning man's authenticity. They forcibly carry out criminal law and engage in punitive expeditions, destroying human lives. This causes people to pursue what is nonessential and to forget what is fundamental, which complicates the emotions and shortens the lifespan. Misled and deluded, they cause deaths, and a return to the past is now impossible. This is the fault of those called "sages."

明本

夫所謂本者，無為之為心也，形骸依之以立也，其為常而不
殆也。如火之可用以焚，不可奪其炎也。如水之可用以潤，
不可奪其濕也。取之不有，藏之不無。動之則察秋毫之形，
審蚊蚋之音；靜之則不見丘山，不聞雷霆。大之可以包天
壤，細之可以入眉睫。惚惚恍恍，不來不往。希希夷夷，不
盈不虧。巢由之隱，園綺之遁，專其根而獨善也，堯授舜，
舜授禹，禹授啟，湯放桀，武王伐紂，張其機而兼濟也。明
之者，可藏則藏，可行則行，應物立事，曠乎無情。昧之
者，嗜欲是馳，耳目是隨，終日妄用，不識不知。孰能照以
無滯之光，委以自然之和，則無名之元，見乎無見之中矣。

19 Inspired by *Daodejing* 16: "The Way is forever, and though the person decays one is not
    endangered" (道乃久，没身不殆).
20 In *Zhuangzi* 23, Laozi is able to tell what kind of person one is by looking at the space
    between the eyebrows and the eyelashes. See Watson 1968, 252.
21 The wording is reminiscent of *Daodejing* 14 and 21, where attempts are made to describe
    the Way.
22 "Chao and You" are the archetypal hermits Chaofu 巢父 and Xu You 許由, whose lives
    are described in, among other sources, Huangfu Mi's 皇甫謐 (215-282) highly influential
    Lives of Eminent Gentlemen (*Gaoshi zhuan* 高士傳). "Yuan and Qi" are Sir Dongyuan 東

Illuminating the Foundation

What I call "the foundation" is to make nonpurposive action the center. That the tangible body relies on it in order to remain erect means that it is something enduring and not endangered.[19] It is like fire, which you can use to burn things, but whose heat you cannot take away. It is like water, which you can use to moisten things, but whose wetness you cannot take away. Try to seize it, and you will not possess it. Be oblivious of it, and you will never be without it.[viii] When you put it in motion, you will be able to scrutinize the shape of the autumnal down of birds, and to closely investigate the sounds made by mosquitoes and blackflies. When you make it motionless, you will not see hills and mountains, nor hear the crash of thunder. Magnifying it enables you to envelop heaven and earth; minimizing it enables you to enter between the eyebrows and eyelashes.[20] Indistinct, it neither comes nor goes; imperceptible, it neither waxes nor wanes.[21]

That Chao and You went into hiding and Yuan and Qi withdrew means that they concentrated on the root and improved themselves in isolation. That Yao handed over the throne to Shun, Shun to Yu, and Yu to Qi, and that Tang banished Jie and King Wu attacked Zhòu means that they deployed their skills and brought succor to all alike.[22][ix]

Those who have grasped this insight can hide when hiding is permissible, and can act when acting is permissible. In response to the exterior world, they will establish things and will be unrestricted because of their absence of partial emotions. Those who are ignorant of this will only pursue what they desire, and follow only their ears and eyes. All the days of their lives will be trifled away, without reaching insight or understanding.[x]

Whoever is able to shine with an unobstructed glow and to entrust himself to the harmony of naturalness will be shown the nameless beginning in the midst of what cannot be seen![xi]

園公 and Qili Ji 綺里季, two of the so-called "four hoaryheads" (*sihao* 四皓), the Qin and early Han hermits who are the protagonists of the chapter "Discourse on the Hermits of Shang" in Book II. Yao 堯 and Shun 舜 are legendary rulers of the ancient predynastic period. Yu 禹 and his son Qi 啓 were the first rulers of the Xia dynasty (21st c. BC?); Tang 湯 established the Shang dynasty (16th c. BC) and King Wu 武王 established the Zhou (11th c. BC). Jie 桀 and Zhòu 紂 are the proverbially evil and cruel last rulers of the Xia and the Shang dynasty respectively.

析惑

夫性者神也，命者氣也，相須於虛無，相生於自然，猶乎塤篪之相感也，陰陽之相和也。形骸者，性命之器也。猶乎火之在薪，薪非火不焚，火非薪不光。形骸非性命不立，性命假形骸以顯，則性命自然沖而生者也，形骸自然滯而死者也。自然生者，雖寂而常生。自然死者，雖搖而常死。

今人莫不好生惡死，而不知自然生死之理，覩乎不搖而偃者則憂之。役其自然生者，務存其自然死者，存之愈切，生之愈疎。是欲沈羽而浮石者也，何惑之甚歟！

23 One's inborn nature (*xing* 性) and one's heaven-ordained lifespan (*ming* 命) together form *xingming* 性命, which in modern Chinese has come to mean simply 'life.'

24 The flutes are an allusion to the ode "What man was that?" (*He ren si* 何人斯) in the *Classic of Poetry*.

25 This passage is quoted in the *Constraints and Efforts in Elucidating the Meaning of the Four Books* (*Sishu jiangyi kunmian lu* 四書講義困勉錄) by the early Qing dynasty Neo-confucian scholar and calligrapher Lu Longqi 陸隴其 (1630–1692). See Lu Longqi, *Siku quanshu* ed., vol. 209, p. 793.

26 The separation between what will die and what cannot die is probably inspired by the first *Liezi* chapter: "Hence there are the begotten and the Begetter of the begotten ... What begetting begets dies, but the Begetter of the begotten never ends." See Graham 1960, 20; Yang Bojun 1985, 10.

Analyzing the Delusion

One's inborn nature is the spiritual essence, and one's heavenly-ordained lifespan is the *qi*.[23] They are mutually dependent upon each other within Void and Nullity, and they generate one another in naturalness, as the vessel-flute and the bamboo cross-flute affect each other, or as yin and yang harmonize with one another.[24]

The tangible body is the utensil of one's inborn nature and heavenly-ordained lifespan. Compare it with fire in firewood: without fire, the firewood will not be set ablaze, and without firewood, the fire will not glow. Without the inborn nature and heavenly-ordained lifespan, the tangible body will not remain erect, while the inborn nature and the heavenly-ordained lifespan rely on the tangible body to manifest themselves.[25] Thus, the inborn nature and heavenly-ordained lifespan are generated by spontaneously bubbling up, whereas the tangible body is dead as a result of spontaneous stagnation. That which is spontaneously generated may be unmoving, but it will always be alive. That which is spontaneously dead may be moving, but it will always be dead.[26 xii]

Now, there are no humans who are not fond of life and do not abhor death. However, they do not understand the principle of what is spontaneously alive or dead. When they behold someone unmoving and supine, they grieve. They subdue that which is spontaneously alive in them, all the while working hard to preserve that which is spontaneously dead.[27] The more ardently they try to preserve the tangible body, the more they are separated from life. This is like a desire to make feathers sink or rocks float.[viii] How serious is their delusion![28 xiv]

---

27 That which is spontaneously dead is the tangible body.

28 Master Incapable recognizes that the tangible body and the life-force cooperate intimately, as the one cannot exist without the other, but he considers the first as naturally dead and the second as naturally alive. Immortality is not explicitly mentioned here, but this chapter can undoubtedly be read as critical of the search for physical immortality, an ambition which in Master Incapable's view must be absurd, for how could one perpetuate something that was originally dead? In particular, the line "the more ardently they try to preserve the tangible body, the more they are separated from life" can easily be understood as being targeted at certain ninth-century emperors who died of alchemical poisoning.

無憂

夫人大惡者死也，形骸不搖而僵者也。夫形骸血肉耳目不能
虛而靈，則非生之具也。故不待不搖而僵則曰死，方搖而趨
本死矣。所以搖而趨者，憑於本不死者耳。非能自搖而趨
者。形骸本死，則非今死；非今死，無死矣。死者，人之大
惡也。無死可惡，則形骸之外，何足泪吾之至和哉？

---

29 The final sentence is inspired by *Daodejing* 13: "The reason we have great worries is that
    we have bodies; if we did not have bodies, what would there be to worry about" (吾所
    以有大患者，為吾有身也，及吾無身，吾有何患)?

Being Free of Worries

People greatly abhor dying, the state wherein the body is unmoving and supine. Now, if the body, the blood, the flesh, the ears, and the eyes could not be void and therefore numinous, they would not be the instruments of life. Therefore, we need not wait until a body is unmoving and supine before we can call it "dead": what hurries on now was originally dead! In order to hurry on, it relied on something originally not dead. It was not able to hurry on out of itself.

If the body is originally dead, that means that it cannot die now, and if it cannot die now, there is no dying! Dying is what people greatly abhor. But if there is no dying to be abhorred, what then, aside from the body, could disturb our utmost harmony?[29][xv]

質妄

一

天下人所共趨之而不知止者，富貴與美名爾。

　　所謂富貴者，足於物爾。夫富貴之亢極者，大則帝王，
小則公侯而已。豈不以被袞冕、處宮闕、建羽葆警蹕，故謂
之帝王耶？豈不以戴簪纓、喧車馬、仗旌旄鈇鉞，故謂之公
侯耶？不飾之以袞冕宮闕羽荷警蹕、簪纓車馬鈇鉞，又何有
乎帝王公侯哉？夫袞冕羽葆、簪纓鈇鉞、旌旄車馬，皆物
也。物足則富貴，富貴則帝王公侯。故曰富貴者足物爾。

　　夫物者，人之所能為者也，自為之，反為不為者感之。
乃以足物者為富貴，無物者為貧賤，於是樂富貴，恥貧賤，
不得其樂者，無所不至，自古及今，醒而不悟。壯哉物之力
也！

　　夫所謂美名者，豈不以居家孝、事上忠、朋友信、臨財
廉、充乎才、足乎藝之類耶？此皆所謂聖人者尚之，以拘愚
人也。

30 Alternative translation: "But from the moment humans make them themselves . . ."

Offering Proof of Fraudulence

I

People under heaven all run toward wealth, noble status, and good reputation, without knowing how to stop. What we call wealth and noble
status amount to having more than enough material things. Of those at
the highest pinnacle of wealth and noble status, the greater are emperors
and princes, and the lesser are dukes and marquises. Is it not because they
wear imperial robes and coronets, reside in palaces, and install feather
baldachins and imperial retinues that we call them emperors or princes?
Is it not because they wear a hatpin and throat-band, create a din with
their horse and carriage, and brandish banners and battle-axes that we
call them dukes and marquises? If they were not adorned with imperial
robes, coronets, palaces, feather baldachins, imperial retinues, hatpins,
throat-bands, horses, carriages and battle-axes, then what would be left
of emperors, princes, dukes and marquises?

Imperial robes, coronets, feather baldachins, hatpins, throat-bands,
battle-axes, banners, horses and carriages are all material things. He who
has more than enough material things has wealth and noble status, and he
who has wealth and status becomes emperor, prince, duke, or marquis.
Therefore, I have said that wealth and noble status amount to having more
than enough material things.

Material things are things that people are capable of producing. But from
the moment they are produced, they are relished by those who did not produce them.[30] Thereupon, those who have more than enough material things
are considered wealthy and noble, and those who are without material things
are considered poor and humble. Henceforth, one takes pleasure in wealth
and noble status, and one feels ashamed because of poverty and humbleness.
Those who do not obtain what is pleasurable will stop at nothing. From the
olden days until today, people have been awake without being aware. How
strong the power of material things is!

What we call a good reputation comes from things such as behaving
with filial piety toward family, being loyal in service of superiors, being
trustworthy to friends, being incorruptible in the presence of riches, being
abundantly talented, and having more than enough skillfulness, does it not?
Those who are called "sages" hold all these things in high esteem, and use
them to restrain the ignorant.

夫何以被之美名者，人之形質爾。無形質，廓乎太空，故非
毀譽所能加也。形質者，囊乎血輿乎滓者也，朝合而暮壞，
何有於美名哉？今人莫不失自然正性而趨之，以至於詐偽激
者，何也？所謂聖人者誤之也。

二

古今之人，謂其所親者血屬，於是情有所專焉。聚則相歡，
離則相思，病則相憂，死則相哭。夫天下之人，與我所親：
手足腹背，耳目口鼻，頭頸眉髮，一也。何以分別乎彼我
哉？所以彼我者，必名字爾。所以疎於天下之人者，不相熟
爾。所以親於所親者，相熟爾。

　　嗟乎！手足腹背，耳目口鼻，頭頸眉髮，俾乎人人離析
之，各求其謂之身體者，且無所得，誰謂所親耶？誰謂天下
之人耶？取於名字彊為者也。若以名所親之名，名天下之
人，則天下之人皆所親矣。若以熟所親之熟，熟天下之人，
則天下之人皆所親矣，胡謂情所專耶？夫無所孝慈者，孝慈
天下；有所孝慈者，孝慈一家。一家之孝慈未弊，則以情相
苦，而孝慈反為累矣。弊則偽，偽則父子兄弟將有嫌怨者
矣。

31　*Xingzhi* 形質 refers to the tangible body.

But what are the carriers of this good reputation? One's outward form and substance.[31] Without outward form and substance, one would be more vast than the universe, and therefore something to which neither blame nor praise could be attached. The outward form and substance are a bag filled with blood, a vehicle for dregs. In the morning it is unified, but as night falls it disintegrates. So of what significance is a good reputation?

Why is it that among people today, there are none who do not run toward a good reputation, thereby losing their spontaneity and correct inborn nature, and being stimulated to act with deception and hypocrisy? Because those called "sages" have led them into error.

II

People both past and present refer to their relatives as their blood-kin, at which point the emotions start to lead. When people gather together, they take pleasure in one another and when they are separated, they long for one another. If they get sick, they feel concerned for one another, and when one of them dies, they bemoan each other. However you look at it, all people under heaven are related to me. We all have hands, feet, belly, back, ears, eyes, mouth, nose, head, neck, eyebrows, and hair. How do we distinguish "the other" from "me"? It must be the name that distinguishes me from the other. We consider ourselves separate from other people under heaven because we are not familiar with them. We feel related to our relatives because we are familiar with them.

Suppose we cut off the hands, feet, bellies, backs, ears, eyes, mouths, noses, heads, necks, eyebrows, and hair of all people under heaven, and have everyone look for what they called their "own body." It would be an impossible task. Whom would you refer to as "your relatives"? And whom would you refer to as "the other people"? It would all be the result of the forcible application of names. If you were to call everyone the name you use for your relatives, then everyone would be your relative! If you were to treat everyone with the same familiarity you treat your relatives with, then all people under heaven would be your relatives! Then how could the emotions lead?

If there is no one in particular to treat with filial devotion and tenderness, then everyone may be treated with filial devotion and tenderness. When there is a particular group to be treated with filial devotion and tenderness, then it is kept within a single family. If filial devotion and tenderness are not exhausted within that family, people make one another miserable with their emotions, and filial devotion and tenderness become burdens. If filial devotion and tenderness are exhausted, there is hypocrisy, and where there is hypocrisy, fathers and sons, and older and younger brothers will start to mistrust and loathe one another.

　　莊子曰：魚相處於陸，相煦以沫，不如相忘於江湖。至哉是言也！夫魚相忘於江湖，人相忘於自然，各適矣。故情有所專者，明者不為。

32　The target of Master Incapable's criticism is the Confucian tendency to translate certain key values predominantly in the context of the family or clan. This brand of particularism had already drawn sharp criticism from Mozi 墨子 (c. 470–c. 391 BC), who demanded "universal affection" (*jian'ai* 兼愛, see, e.g., De Bary and Bloom 1999, 69–72). Master Incapable's standpoint may at times seem influenced by Mohism, but its basis is found in Daoism. "Perfect humaneness is free of affection" (至仁无親) states *Zhuangzi* 14, referring to the affection that exists between relatives. And in *Daodejing* 79 we read: "The Way of heaven [or nature] is free of kinship-based affection" (天道無親). *Daodejing* 18 traces the birth of filial devotion and the kindness shown by parents to their children back to the loss of harmony between the different kinships: "When the six kinships are no longer harmonious, filial devotion and tenderness arise" (六親不和，有孝慈).

Zhuangzi says: "When the fish are left stranded side by side on the ground, they spit foam at each other—but it would be much better if they could be oblivious of one another in the rivers and lakes."[xvi] These words are perfect! Just as it is appropriate for fish to forget one another in rivers and lakes, it is appropriate for humans to be oblivious of one another in what-is-so-of-itself! Therefore, those who are enlightened do not let emotions lead them.[32][xvii]

真修

一

夫衡鏡，物也，成於人者也。人自成之，而反求輕重於衡、
妍醜於鏡者，何也？衡無心而平，鏡無心而明也。

　　夫無心之物，且平且明，則夫民之有心者，研之以無；
澄之以虛，涵澈希夷，不知所如，吾見其偕天壤以無疆，淪
顥然而不疲，而天下莫能與之爭矣。

二

夫水之性，壅之則澄，決之則流，昇之雲則雨，沈之土則
潤，為江海而不務其大，在坎穴而不恥其小，分百川而不
疲，利萬物而不辭，至柔者也。故老聃曰：柔弱勝剛彊。

33 Nullity, the Void, the Inaudible, and the Invisible are all qualities associated with
    the Way.
34 The last part of this sentence is a quote from *Daodejing* 22 and 66: "It is because the Sage
    does not compete that no one under heaven will be able to compete with him" (夫唯不爭
    ，故天下莫能與之爭). Zhang Songhui (2005, 46) is correct in pointing out that *Master
    Incapable* may also have been influenced here by a passage in chapter 20 of *Zhuangzi*,
    where being empty is described as a means of being protected from harm (人能虛己以
    遊世，其孰能害之). See Watson 1968, 212; Guo Qingfan 1985, 675.

True Cultivation

I

The balance and the mirror are material things, and they are shaped by people. From the moment people shaped them, they have sought in turn to know light and heavy from the balance, and beauty and ugliness from the mirror. Why is this so? It is because the balance is free of intentionality and thus impartial, and because the mirror is free of intentionality and thus bright.[xviii]

If objects that are without intentionality are both impartial and bright, then let this serve as a model for whoever does have intentionality:[xix]

> Grind them through Nullity,
> make them limpid through the Void,
> drench them in the Inaudible and the Invisible,
> so they will not know what they do.[33]

We will see them become companions of heaven and earth in their unboundedness. Engulfed in brilliant white *qi*, they will not grow weary, and no one under heaven will be able to compete with them.[34]

II

This is the inborn nature of water: dam it and it becomes transparent; break the dam and it flows. When it rises up to form clouds, it brings rain, and when it sinks into the soil, it brings moisture. It forms rivers and seas but does not strive to be big. Standing in pits and holes, it does not feel ashamed of its smallness. It divides into a hundred rivers but does not get exhausted. It brings profit to the myriad things and never leaves. It is the epitome of flexibility. Therefore Old Longears said: "The flexible and tender overcomes the hard and strong."[35] Hence, he who contains

---

35 A quote from *Daodejing* 36. Old Longears (Lao Dan 老聃) is how Laozi is often referred to in *Zhuangzi*.

則含神體虛，專氣致柔者，得乎自然之元者也。

三

夫水流濕，火就燥，雲從龍，風從虎，自然感應之理也。故
神之召氣，氣之從神，猶此也。知自然之相應，專玄牝之歸
根，則幾乎懸解矣。

36 The first part of the sentence is a quote from *Daodejing* 10. The *Daodejing* (8, 66, and 78)
   repeatedly praises the qualities of water: it benefits all things without striving and it is
   content with the lowliest position; nothing in the world is softer or more flexible than
   water, yet nothing surpasses it when the hard and strong need to be attacked. Master
   Incapable calls it the epitome of flexibility (*rou* 柔). Bringing about flexibility is here

the Spirit and embodies the Void, who concentrates on the vital energy and produces flexibility, obtains the origin of what-is-so-of-itself.[36][xx]

III

Water flows toward dampness, fire moves toward what is dry, clouds follow the dragon, and wind follows the tiger.[37] That is the principle of spontaneous sympathetic response. Therefore, when Spirit summons the vital energies, and the vital energies follow Spirit, we are talking about the same thing. If you understand the mutual correspondences of what-is-so-of-itself, and you concentrate on the return to the root via the mysterious feminine, then you come very close to being liberated of shackles![38]

considered one of four conditions for "obtaining the origin of what-is-so-of-itself." The other prerequisites are: to concentrate on the vital energy (*qi*), to embody the Void (*xu* 虛), and to contain the Spirit. Different from the Buddhist notion of Emptiness (*kong* 空), the Daoist Void does not indicate the fundamentally illusory nature of all phenomena but rather an unlimited potentiality. Intimately related to Nullity (*wu* 無), the Void enables things to serve as vessels for the subtlest forces. "If the body, the blood, the flesh, the ears, and the eyes could not be void and therefore numinous, they would not be the instruments of life," states *Master Incapable* in "Being Free of Worries." The Void is the ontological stage before that of concretization: an unlimited wealth of possibilities is left open. He who embodies the Void maintains a maximum of potential and is therefore able to make his own naturalness manifest itself.

37 Master Incapable quotes the *Classic of Changes* here, more specifically the commentary to the first hexagram, *qian* 乾. Master Incapable refers to this example of the "principle of spontaneous sympathetic response" (*ziran ganying* 自然感應) in order to point out the relation between Spirit and vital energy, whereby Spirit plays the leading role.

38 The mysterious feminine (*xuanpin* 玄牝) originates in the enigmatic *Daodejing* 6, which opens with the statement that "the spirit of the valley does not die" and that this is the mysterious feminine. "The gate of the mysterious feminine," continues the text, "is what is called the root of heaven and earth." The Heshanggong 河上公 commentary explains "valley" as "to nurture," "spirit" as "the gods of the five inner organs," and the mysterious feminine as the mouth and nose, since it is through the mouth and nose that nature feeds human beings the five vital energies. The probably roughly contemporary Xiang'er 想爾 commentary, on the other hand, explains "valley" as "desire," and the gate of the mysterious feminine as the vagina. In spite of all this lexical uncertainty, it seems safe to conclude that what is described here is a technique of "nourishing life" (*yangsheng* 養生) based on feminine vital energy. Being "liberated of shackles" or "freed of the bonds" (*xuanjie* 懸解) is a notion originating in the third *Zhuangzi* chapter, in the context of the equanimity in the face of death. He who comprehends that life and death are but two aspects of the same natural process is no longer torn between conflicting emotions such as joy and sorrow, and is therefore freed.

四

夫鳥飛於空，魚游於淵，非術也，自然而然也。故為鳥為魚
者，亦不自知其能飛能游。苟知之，立心以為之，則必墮必
溺矣。亦猶人之足馳手捉、耳聽目視，不待習而能之也。當
其馳捉聽視之際，應機自至，又不待思而施之也。苟須思之
而後可施之，則疲矣。是以任自然者久，得其常者濟。夫浩
然而虛者，心之自然也。今人手足耳目，則任其自然而馳捉
聽視焉。至於心，則不任其自然而撓焉，欲其至和而靈通也
難矣。

IV

Birds fly in the air and fish swim in the deep, not through some special technique, but rather through what-is-so-of-itself. Therefore, a bird or a fish has no self-knowledge of the ability to fly or swim. If birds and fish did have this knowledge, and if they were to set their minds on performing these actions, then they would certainly fall or drown.

This also applies to people, who run with their feet, grasp with their hands, listen with their ears, and look with their eyes. They are capable of doing these things without being dependent on practice. When one is running, grasping, listening, and watching, one arrives at these actions out of oneself, in response to circumstances, and is not dependent on thought to carry them out. If thought were needed to be able to carry them out, it would be exhausting! For this reason, he who relies on spontaneity will last, and he who obtains constancy will be saved.

It is the spontaneous nature of the mind to be flood-like and empty. Now, when people use their hands, feet, ears, and eyes, they rely on spontaneity to grasp, run, listen, and look. As far as the mind is concerned, however, they do not rely on spontaneity and instead disturb it. That way, longing for utmost harmony and supernatural communication is impossible![xxi]

BOOK II
无能子卷中

文王說

呂望釣於渭濱，西伯將畋，筮之。其繇曰："非熊非羆，天
遣爾師。"及畋得望，西伯再拜，望釣不輟。西伯拜不止，
望箕踞笑曰："汝何為來哉？"

　　西伯曰："殷政荒矣，生民荼矣，愚將拯之，思得賢
士。"

　　望曰："殷政自荒，生民自荼，胡與於汝，汝胡垢予。"

　　西伯曰："夫聖人不藏用以獨善於己，必盡智以兼濟萬
物，豈無是耶？"

　　望曰："夫人與鳥獸昆蟲，共浮於天地中，一炁而已。
猶乎天下城郭屋舍，皆峙於空虛者也。盡壞城郭屋舍，其空
常空。若盡殺人及鳥獸昆蟲，其炁常炁。殷政何能荒耶？生
民何謂荼耶？雖然，城郭屋舍已成不必壞，

1　King Wen, the "Civilizing King," is the posthumous title of Ji Chang 姬昌 (1112?–1050
BC). Although it was his son who terminated the Shang dynasty, Ji Chang was honored
as the founding king of the Zhou. In Master Incapable's text, he is named Xi Bo, or
"Count of the West," the title he had received from his sovereign, the last Shang king,
whom he would later overthrow. Lü Wang, literally "the hope from Lü," is one of many
appellations of Jiang Shang 姜尚, also known as Jiang Ziya 姜子牙, Taigong Wang 太公
望 ("Grand Duke Hope") and Qi Taigong 齊太公 ("Grand Duke from Qi"). A nobleman
from what would later become the state of Qi, he assisted the future first two Zhou kings
in overthrowing the Shang dynasty. On Lü Wang, see Allan 1972–1973.

Discourse on King Wen

Lü Wang was fishing on the bank of the River Wei.[1] As the Count of the West was about to go hunting, he divined using yarrow stalks. The interpretation of the hexagram read: "Neither a black bear nor a brown bear is he; heaven bequeaths you a teacher."[2] While hunting, the Count of the West came upon Wang. He bowed repeatedly, but Wang went on fishing without interruption. The Count of the West continued bowing with respect, until Wang, who sat with his legs stretched out, said with a smile, "Why did you come here?"[3]

The Count of the West said, "The government of Yin has fallen to ruin.[4] The people suffer cruelly! I humbly intend to rescue them, and to do so, I think I should find a worthy man."

Wang said, "The government of Yin has fallen to ruin because of itself; the living people are suffering because of themselves. What have you got to do with it? And why sully me with it?"

"However you look at it," said the Count of the West, "a sagely man does not conceal his usefulness with the aim of improving himself in isolation. Instead he will exhaust his knowledge to give succor to the myriad things without distinction. Is that not so?"

Wang said, "Along with the birds, the beasts, and the masses of insects, humans float between heaven and earth, sharing the same *qi*, and that's all there is to it. This is like the cities and houses in the empire, which all stand in the void. You may destroy all the cities and houses, but the void will always remain the void. Even if you kill off all the humans, birds, beasts, and insects, the *qi* will always be the *qi*. How could the government of Yin be neglected? Why claim that the people are suffering? Nevertheless, once the cities and houses have been built, there's no need

2   In other words, this teacher will lack a martial appearance.
3   Lü Wang makes no attempt to be polite towards the future Zhou ruler. He addresses the Count as *ru* 汝 (used to address social inferiors or people one wants to belittle), he continues fishing (as Zhuangzi is said to have done when the king of Chu unsuccessfully offered him the post of minister, in *Zhuangzi* 17), and he sits spreadeagled, a clear sign of disrespect (again echoing Zhuangzi, when visited by fellow philosopher Hui Shi after the death of Zhuangzi's wife, in *Zhuangzi* 18).
4   The Shang dynasty was called Yin after its capital was moved to that city.

生民已形不必殺，予將拯之矣。"乃許西伯同載而歸。

太顛閎夭私於西伯曰："公劉后稷之積德累功，以及於王，王之德充乎祖宗矣。今三分天下，王有其二，亦可謂隆矣。呂望漁者爾，王何謂下之甚耶？"

西伯曰："夫無為之德，包裹天地；有為之德，開物成事。軒轅陶唐之為天子也，以有為之德，謁廣成子於崆峒，叩許由於箕山，而不獲其一顧。矧吾之德，未迨乎軒堯，而卑無為之德乎？"

太顛閎夭曰："如王之說，望固無為之德也，何謂從王之有為耶？"

西伯曰："天地無為也，日月星辰，運於晝夜，雨露霜雪，零於秋冬，江河流而不息，草木生而不止，故無為則能無滯。若滯於有為，則不能無為矣。"

呂望聞之，知西伯實於憂民，不利於得殷天下，於是乎卒與之興周焉。

5   Taidian and Hongyao are two of King Wen's ministers.The legendary culture hero Houji 后稷 (Sovereign Millet), considered to be the ancestor of the Zhou, was also venerated as the god of harvests. Gong Liu 公劉 (Duke Liu) was his great-grandson. He is said to have led the ancestors of the Zhou people back to a sedentary life of agriculture after a period of nomadic hunting and gathering.
6   Xuanyuan 軒轅 is Huangdi, the Yellow Emperor; Taotang 陶唐 is the clan name of the legendary sage-king Yao.

to destroy them.[xxii] Once people have taken form, there's no need to kill them. I will come to their rescue!" Whereupon he gave his permission to the Count of the West, and both returned in the same carriage.

Taidian and Hongyao privately said to the Count of the West, "The accumulated virtue and the successive achievements of Duke Liu and Houji have been passed on to you, King.[5] The King's virtue is more abundant than that of your ancestors! The King now possesses two-thirds of all under heaven, and that deserves to be called a triumph! Lü Wang, on the other hand, is but a fisherman. Why would the King lower himself so far?"[xxiii]

The Count of the West said, "The virtue of nonpurposive action surrounds heaven and earth; the virtue of purposive action inaugurates and completes things. That Xuanyuan and Taotang became Son of Heaven was thanks to the virtue of purposive action.[6] Xuanyuan paid his respects to Guangchengzi on Mount Kongtong, and Taotang interrogated Xu You on Mount Ji, but they did not get their attention.[7] As far as my virtue is concerned, it is no match for that of Xuanyuan or Yao, so how would I dare to look down upon the virtue of nonpurposive action?"[xxiv]

Taidian and Hongyao said, "If it is as the King says, then Lü Wang assuredly possesses the virtue of nonpurposive action. But why then would he comply with the King's purposive action?"

"Heaven and Earth do not undertake purposive action," said the Count of the West. "The sun, moon, and stars revolve day and night. Rain, dew, frost, and snow gently fall in autumn and winter.[xxv] Rivers flow without resting, and plants grow unceasingly. Therefore, it is through the absence of purposive action that absence of stagnation becomes possible. If one is obstructed by purposive action, one is unable to engage in nonpurposive action!"

When Lü Wang heard this, he understood that the Count of the West was sincere in his concern for the people, and that he was not looking for profit in obtaining the empire of Yin. So he took the lead and helped him make Zhou flourishing and strong.[8][xxvi]

7 The conversation between the Yellow Emperor and the wise hermit Guangchengzi 廣成子 ("Master Broadrange Complete" in Ziporyn 2020) is recounted in *Zhuangzi* 11 (Watson 1968, 118–120); Yao's unsuccessful attempt to cede the empire to Xu You, the archetypal recluse, is described in the first *Zhuangzi* chapter (see Watson 1968, 32–33).

8 Because the hermit Lü Wang in the end helps King Wen overthrow the Shang dynasty, this chapter has been considered a breakdown of Master Incapable's anarchist thought. See Hsiao 1936, 262 and Rapp 1978, 94–97. The original anecdote is in Nienhauser 1994–2019, vol. V.1, 31-38; *Records of the Historian* 32.1477-1478.

首陽子說

文王歿，武王伐紂，滅之。伯夷叔齊叩馬諫曰：“父死不
葬，而起大事，動大眾，非孝也。為臣弒君，非忠也。”左
右欲兵之，武王義而釋之。伯夷叔齊乃反，隱首陽山，號首
陽子。

　　夫天下自然之時，君臣無分乎其間。為之君臣以別尊
卑，謂之聖人者以智欺愚也。以智欺愚，妄也。吾與汝嘗言
之矣。妄為君臣之中，妄殷有稱。妄殷之中，妄辛有稱。妄
辛之中，妄暴妄虐，以充妄欲。姬發之動，亦欲也。欲則
妄，所謂以妄取妄者也。夫無為則淳正而當天理，

9   Zhòu 紂 is the common appellation of the last ruler of the Shang or Yin dynasty. Refer-
    ring to the leather strap tied from a horse's rump to carriage shafts, it was meant as an
    insult. Zhòu is portrayed as extraordinarily evil and cruel, organizing orgies, inventing
    horrible forms of torture, and killing or imprisoning virtuous relatives. All of this was
    probably somewhat exaggerated by Zhou historiographers in order to provide a neat
    contrast with the "noble rebels" who founded the new dynasty. The real name of King
    Wu ("the martial king"), son of King Wen, was Ji Fa 姬發.

Discourse on the Masters of Shouyang

When King Wen died, King Wu attacked Zhòu and destroyed him.[9] Bo Yi and Shu Qi grabbed hold of the king's horse and admonished him: "Your father is dead and not yet buried, and yet you set up a great enterprise and mobilize a huge crowd. That is not filial devotion. As a subject you murder your ruler. That is not loyalty."[10] The king's attendants wanted to raise their weapons against them, but King Wu, considering them right-minded, let them go. So Bo Yi and Shu Qi returned and withdrew to Mount Shouyang. They were called the Masters of Shouyang.[11]

When all-under-heaven was in its natural state, there was no distinction between rulers and subjects. That rulers and subjects were created so as to separate the venerable from the lowly means that those called "sages" used their knowledge to deceive the ignorant. Using one's knowledge to deceive the ignorant is fraudulence.[xxvii] Let me attempt to explain![12] Amid fraudulent rulers and subjects, the fraudulent Yin deserves mention. Amid the fraudulent Yin, the fraudulent Xin deserves mention.[13] At the heart of the fraudulent Xin were fraudulent violence and fraudulent cruelty, as a means to satisfy fraudulent desires.[xxviii] Ji Fa's actions were also inspired by desire, and desire leads to fraudulence. That is what we call "fraudulence begets fraudulence." When there is no purposive action, humans are uncorrupted and correct, and accord

---

10 The legendary hermits Bo Yi 伯夷 ("Elder brother Yi") and Shu Qi 叔齊 ("Third brother Qi") were the sons of the king of the small state of Guzhu 孤竹. When the old king wanted his younger son to inherit the throne, Bo Yi left in order not to be in the way of Shu Qi. Shu Qi himself also left because he was convinced his older brother should become the new ruler. The brothers became famous for their refusal to "eat the grain of the new Zhou dynasty" (for in their eyes, the future Zhou kings were traitors who rebelled against their sovereign), and because they were repeatedly mentioned in the *Analects* as men who would not "bend their wills." Bo Yi and Shu Qi are conspicuously absent from *Lives of Eminent Gentlemen*.

11 In the following paragraph, it is Master Incapable himself who addresses Bo Yi and Shu Qi.

12 I take *chang* 嘗 to mean "attempt" here. An alternative, though less plausible, translation would be: "I once explained this to you."

13 Xin 辛 was the actual name of the tyrant Zhòu.

父子君臣何有哉？有為則嗜欲而亂人性，孝不孝忠不忠何異
哉？今汝妄吾之嘗言，又以妄說突其妄兵，是求義聲也。以
必朽之骨而迎虛聲，是以風掇焰也。姬發不兵汝，幸也。兵
之而得義聲，朽骨何有哉？夫龍暴其鱗，鳳暴其翼，必伺於
漁者弋者。悲乎！殆非吾之友也。

夷齊於是逃入首陽山，罔知所終，後人以為餓死。

---

14 Literally, Heaven's principles (*tianli* 天理).
15 These weapons are those trained on them by the king's attendants.

with the natural order.[14] How would there be any "fathers and sons" or "rulers and subjects"? When there is purposive action, there are cravings and desires, and people's inborn nature is brought into disorder. In that case, it does not matter whether there is filial devotion or not, or there is loyalty or not! Now you think what I am attempting to say is fraudulent, and with your own fraudulent theory you charge at his fraudulent weapons, seeking a reputation for propriety.[15][xxix] Welcoming a false reputation with these bones of yours, which will necessarily rot away, is like putting out a blazing fire with wind. You are lucky Ji Fa is not putting you to death. And if Ji Fa were to kill you, and you were to obtain a reputation for propriety, what good would that do a bunch of rotting bones? When the dragon exposes its scales and the phoenix exposes its wings, they will certainly be spied upon by fishermen and hunters.[xxx] It saddens me, but you will likely not be friends of mine!

Yi and Qi then absconded to Mount Shouyang, but it is unknown how they met their end. Later generations assumed they starved to death.[xxxi]

老君說

孔子定禮樂，明舊章，刪《詩》、《書》，修《春秋》，
將以正人倫之序，杜亂臣賊子之心，往告於老聃。

　老聃曰："夫治大國者若烹小鮮，蹂於刀几則爛矣。自
昔聖人創物立事，誘動人情，人情失於自然，而夭其性命者
紛然矣。今汝又文而緟之，以繁人情。人情繁則怠，怠則
詐，詐則益亂。所謂伐天真而矜己者也，天禍必及。"

　孔子懼，然亦不能遂已。

　既而削跡於衛，伐樹於宋，饑於陳蔡，圍於匡，皇皇汲
汲，幾於不免。孔子顧謂顏回曰："老聃之言，豈是謂乎？"

16 "Lord Lao" is short for Taishang Laojun 太上老君 or "Grand Supreme Lord Lao," as
Laozi (or Old Longears) was called in the Daoist tradition. The *Classic of Poetry* is China's
oldest poetry collection (11th–7th c. BC), said to have been selected by Confucius. The
Classic of Documents purports to contain formal speeches by kings and other figures
of ancient China. The *Spring and Autumn Annals* is a terse chronicle of the state of Lu
魯 from 722 to 481 BC, traditionally considered to have been compiled by Confucius.
For two thousand years, these three classics have served as models and inspiration for
literature, political philosophy, rhetoric, and education.

Discourse on Lord Lao

Confucius established ritual and music, illuminated the ancient statutes, expurgated the *Classic of Poetry* and the *Classic of Documents*, and compiled the *Spring and Autumn Annals*.[16] In doing so, he wanted to rectify the order in human relationships, and to curb the ambitions of lawless subjects and villainous sons. He went to announce this to Old Longears.

Old Longears said: "However you look at it, governing a large state is like cooking small fish.[17] If you crush them on the chopping block, they fall apart. Since the sages of long ago created things and established tasks, they have been eliciting and exciting man's emotions. Human emotions have lost their naturalness, and there has been a profusion of lives cut short! Now you further civilize them and render them more elaborate, thereby increasing the complexity of human emotions. An increase in the complexity of human emotions leads to insolence, insolence leads to duplicity, and duplicity leads to more disorder. This is what we call attacking natural authenticity while bragging. Heaven is bound to send calamities down upon you."

Confucius became frightened, but was unable to follow Laozi's advice.

Not long afterward, his footprints were erased in Wei, and in Song, people chopped down the tree under which he sat. He starved in Chen and Cai, and he was surrounded in Kuang.[18] Unsettled and anxious, he nearly didn't escape his predicament. Confucius looked at Yan Hui and said, "Would this be what Old Longears was talking about?"[19] xxxii

---

17 A quotation from *Daodejing* 60.

18 The trials and tribulations of Confucius during his wandering years following his exile from his home state of Lu are not only described in the biographical accounts in *Records of the Historian* 47 and 67, but also referred to in *Zhuangzi* 31 and *Liezi* 7, which served as direct sources of inspiration for Master Incapable. Of course, Confucian sources do not mention that Confucius' hardships had anything to do with what Laozi might have told him.

19 Yan Hui was a favorite disciple of Confucius.

孔子說

一

孔子圍於匡，七日絃歌不輟。

　　子路曰：“由聞君子包周身之防，無一朝之患。夫子聖人也，而饑於陳，圍於匡，何也？然而夫子絃歌不輟，罔有憂色，豈有術乎？”

　　孔子曰：“由來，語汝，夫是非邪正由乎人，厚薄懸乎分，通塞存乎時。日月之照，不能免薄蝕之患。聖賢之智，不能移厚薄通塞之數。君子能仁於人，不能使人仁於我。我能義於人，不能使人義於我。匡之圍，非丘之罪也，丘亦不能使之不圍焉。然而可圍者，丘之形骸也。丘方惚無形於沖漠，淪無情於杳冥，不知所以憂，故偶諧於絃歌爾。”

　　言未幾，匡人解去。

20 The people of Kuang had earlier suffered at the hands of a man who resembled Confucius.
    When Confucius passed through the region, people mistook him for the evildoer and
    surrounded him.

21 Zilu 子路 was the style name of Zhong You 仲由 (542–480), one of Confucius' best
    known disciples.

Discourses on Confucius

I

While Confucius was surrounded in Kuang, he strummed the zither and sang for seven days straight.[20]

Zilu said, "I have heard that a gentleman protects himself so that he need not worry even for a single morning. You, Master, are a sagely man, and yet you went hungry in Chen, and you are being surrounded in Kuang. Why is that? Yet even so, you keep strumming the zither and singing, seemingly untroubled. Do you have some technique for this?"[21]

"Come here and I will tell you," said Confucius. "Others decide what is considered right or wrong and unorthodox or orthodox. Whether you're treated generously or poorly depends on allotment.[xxxiii] Whether you are impeded or not depends on the times. The radiance of the sun and moon cannot prevent the calamity of an eclipse. The wisdom of the sages and the worthy cannot change whether one's lot is to be treated generously or poorly, or be impeded or not.[xxxiv] The gentleman can be humane towards others, but he cannot make others behave humanely towards him. He can treat others with propriety, but he cannot make others treat him with propriety.[22] I cannot be held accountable for the fact that I am being surrounded in Kuang, and I cannot keep them from surrounding me. Even so, it is my tangible body that can be surrounded. Just now, I was formless in emptiness and silence. Free of emotions, I was immersed in unfathomable darkness. I know of nothing to be anxious about and amuse myself by strumming the zither and singing."

Soon after, the people of Kuang lifted their siege and left.[23]

22 A similar line of reasoning is found in the conclusion to the chapter "Being Certain of Oneself" (*Bi ji* 必己) in *Mr. Lü's Spring and Autumn Annals*.

23 Master Incapable's inspiration is an anecdote in *Zhuangzi* 17 (see Watson 1968, 184–185; Guo Qingfan 1985, 595–597). But whereas the *Zhuangzi* anecdote is essentially a lesson on the acceptance of fate, Master Incapable points at the difference between body and mind. Whereas the body may be surrounded, the mind has the freedom to move unhindered. The description of Confucius being "formless in emptiness and silence," and "free of emotions and immersed in unfathomable darkness" comes close to Master Incapable's ideal of no-mind.

二

原憲居陋巷，子貢方相魯衛，結騎聯駟訪憲焉。憲攝弊衣。

　　子貢曰："夫子病耶？"

　　憲曰："憲聞德義不修謂之病，無財謂之貧。憲貧也，
非病也。"

　　子貢恥其言，終身不敢復見憲。

　　仲尼聞之曰："賜也言失之也。夫拘於形者不虛，存於
心者不淳，不虛則思之不清，不淳則其心不貞。賜近於驕
欲，憲近於堅白，比之清濁，將去幾何！"

24 Like Yan Hui in a previous chapter, Yuan Xian is another of Confucius' disciples and has
    a biographical sketch in *Lives of Eminent Gentlemen*. Zigong 子貢 is the style name of
    Duanmu Ci 端木賜 (520–456), a businessman and diplomat who occupied a number of
    high government posts. He is considered one of the most important and faithful disciples
    of Confucius.

II

Yuan Xian lived in a narrow alley. Zigong, who was minister in Lu and Wey at the time, went to visit Xian with a whole team of horses and carriages.[24][xxxv] Xian clutched at his tattered clothes.

"Are you ill?" Zigong said.

Xian said, "I have heard that not cultivating virtue and propriety is called an illness, and that having no possessions is called poverty. I am poor, but not ill."

Zigong was ashamed of what he had said, and for the rest of his days he dared not go to see Xian again.

When Confucius heard of this, he said, "Ci really said the wrong thing! One who is stuck on outward appearances is not empty; one who keeps things in the mind is not pure. When one is not empty, one's thoughts will not be clear, and when one is not pure, one's mind is not chaste. Ci is inclined to be arrogant and desirous, whereas Xian is inclined to be 'hard and white.' If one compares them in terms of who is clear and who is muddied, the difference between them is substantial!"[25]

25 Once more, Master Incapable is inspired by a *Zhuangzi* anecdote, this time from chapter 28 (see Watson 1968, 315–316; Guo Qingfan 1985, 975–977). But whereas *Zhuangzi* concludes with the words of Yuan Xian, who explains that he would never change his behavior with the intention of gaining higher status in society, Master Incapable has Confucius make a plea for emptiness and mental purity. The "hard and white" mean integrity and perseverance here, and refer to *Analects* 17.7, where it is said that what is truly hard will not wear even when it is ground, and that what is truly white will not stain even when it is steeped in a dark fluid. A similar anecdote is also found in Nienhauser 1994-2019, vol. VII, 77; *Records of the Historian* 67.2208) but without the presence of Confucius, who had already died when Zigong visited Yuan Xian.

范蠡說

范蠡佐越王勾踐，滅吳殺夫差，與大夫種謀曰："吾聞陰謀
人者，其禍必復。夫姑蘇之滅，夫差之死，由吾與子陰謀
也。況王之為人也，可與共患，不可共樂；且功成、名遂、
身退，天之理也。吾將退，子其偕乎？"

　　大夫種曰："夫天地之於萬物也，春生冬殺，萬物豈於
冬殺而反禍天地乎？吾聞聖人不貴乎獨善，而貴乎除害成
物。苟成於物，除害可也。是以黃帝殺蚩尤，舜去四凶。

---

26 Master Incapable here takes inspiration from *Records of the Historian* 41.1739–1756. Around
    500 BC Wu and Yue were two states on the southeastern periphery of the Chinese world.
    In 494 BC Yue was defeated by Wu but not annihilated. Goujian 勾踐 (r. 496–465 BC),
    king of Yue, secretly built up his forces and occupied Gusu 姑蘇 (present-day Suzhou),
    the capital of the state of Wu, after a surprise attack. Fuchai 夫差 (r. 495–473 BC), king
    of Wu, sought terms, but Fan Li, advisor of Goujian, convinced his king not to agree. In
    473, after Fuchai's suicide, the state of Wu ceased to exist. Grand Master Zhong 大夫種,
    whose real name was Wen Zhong 文種, was another of Goujian's advisors.

Discourse on Fan Li

Fan Li was assisting Goujian, king of Yue. After having destroyed Wu and killed Fuchai, he consulted with Grand Master Zhong.[26] "From what I've heard, the calamities caused by people who secretly plot against others will certainly rebound on them. The destruction of Gusu and Fuchai's death are the result of our secret scheming. As a man, the king is someone with whom one can share misfortune but not enjoyment.[27] Furthermore, when one has accomplished something and made a reputation, it is the Way of nature to withdraw.[28] I am about to withdraw. Will you accompany me?"

Grand Master Zhong said, "Heaven and earth give the myriad beings life in the spring, and in winter they kill them. Still, it is inconceivable that the myriad beings would in turn inflict harm on heaven and earth because they are killed in winter! I have been told that the sagely man does not prize improving himself in solitude, but rather values eliminating what is harmful and establishing things. If one is establishing things, it is permissible to eliminate what is harmful. Therefore, the Yellow Emperor killed Chiyou, and Shun rid himself of the four baleful ones.[29] We

---

27 Master Incapable quotes from the letter (preserved in *Records of the Historian* 41.1746) written by Fan Li to convince Grand Master Zhong to withdraw from politics.

28 Timely withdrawal is one of Laozi's lessons. "When meritorious exploits have been established and one's reputation has consequently been made, it is the Way of heaven [here meaning nature] to withdraw," concludes *Daodejing* 9. Master Incapable puts these words in the mouth of advisor Fan Li, who according to tradition was the disciple of Wenzi 文子, who in his turn is said to have been a disciple of none other than Laozi himself.

29 Chiyou 蚩尤, sometimes depicted as half man, half bull, has been worshipped as a god of war. The Hmong (Miao) consider him their ancestor. Described as a mighty warrior, he was defeated by the Yellow Emperor. See Puett 1998. The Chiyou myths probably go back to the real tribal battles for control of what would become the heartland of Chinese civilization. The four baleful ones (*sixiong* 四凶) are Gonggong 共工 (held responsible for knocking the earth's axis off center and causing disastrous floods), Huandou 驩兜 (the name of a region and a tribe, as well as a minister said to have conspired with Gonggong against Yao), Gun 鯀 (father of Yu the Great, who was unable to control the floods and thus was responsible for the death of countless people), and the Sanmiao 三苗 (the same tribes involved in the Chiyou myths). Gonggong was banished and Gun executed; the others were driven off.

我今除吳之亂，成越之霸，亦成物除害爾，何禍之復我哉？
況王方以滅吳德子與我，必相始終，子無遽於退也！"

范蠡曰："不然，夫天地無心，且不自宰，況宰物乎？
天地自天地，萬物自萬物，春以和自生，冬以寒自殺，非天
地使之然也。聖人雖有心，其用也體乎天地。天地雖無心，
機動則應，事迫則順，事過則逆，除害成物，無所憎愛。故
害除而無禍，物成而無福。今王以怨吳之心，祿我與子以取
其謀。我與子利其祿而謀吳，以滅人為功，以報祿我者。人
之姦也，自謂天地之生殺，聖人之除害成物，不其欺耶？"
大夫種不悅，疑之不決。

范蠡竟辭勾踐，泛扁舟於五湖，俄而越殺大夫種。

30 *Wuxin.*
31 The "Five Lakes" indicate Lake Tai 太湖 and four adjoining lakes in what is now Jiangsu
province. Master Incapable does not mention that, according to one tradition, Fan Li
went to live on a fishing boat with Xi Shi 西施, one of the famous Four Beauties of ancient China. Xi Shi had been given as a present to Fuchai, king of Wu, as the result of
secret scheming between Wen Zhong and Fan Li, who knew the king could not say no
to female beauty and would consequently neglect state affairs, which he did.

have now eliminated the chaos caused by Wu, and we have established Yue as hegemon. We have thus established things and eliminated what was harmful! Why would we be struck by disaster? Moreover, the king has treated us graciously because of the destruction of Wu, and we must remain by his side from beginning to end.[xxxvi] Please don't be so hasty to retire!"

"That's not so," said Fan Li. "Heaven and earth are without intentionality.[30] Moreover, they do not govern themselves, so how could they govern other things? Heaven and earth are heaven and earth in and of themselves; the myriad things are the myriad things in and of themselves. In spring they spontaneously come to life because of the warmth, and in winter they spontaneously kill themselves because of the cold.[xxxvii] It is not that heaven and earth cause this. Even though the sage has intentionality, it is his function to be an embodiment of heaven and earth. And even though heaven and earth are without intentionality, when mechanisms are set in motion, they will respond. When things press forward, they will go along, and when things go too far, they will push back. In eliminating what is harmful and in establishing things, heaven and earth do not hate or love. Therefore, when what was harmful has been eliminated, there is no misfortune, and when things have been established, there is no good fortune. Now the king, with his heart full of resentment for Wu, has paid us a salary so as to obtain our counsel. We both coveted the salary and so we plotted against Wu. In order to recompense the man who paid us our salary, we destroyed others as though it were an honorable achievement. When the most perfidious of men claim they give or take life just like heaven and earth do, and that they eliminate the harmful and establish things just like the sages do, is that not deceit?"

Grand Master Zhong was displeased. Uncertain, he could not come to a decision. In the end, Fan Li took leave of Goujian and went to drift on the Five Lakes in a skiff.[31] Shortly afterwards, Yue executed Grand Master Zhong.[32]

---

32 Wen Zhong was given a sword by his king, or in other words, he was given the honor of committing suicide. See *Records of the Historian* 41.1747.

宋玉說

屈原仕楚，為三閭大夫。楚襄王無德，佞臣靳尚有寵，楚國
不治。屈原憂之，諫襄王請斥靳尚。王不聽，原極諫。

其徒宋玉止之曰：“夫君子之心也，修乎己不病乎人，
晦其用不曜於眾，時來則應，物來則濟，應時而不謀己，濟
物而不務功。是以惠無所歸，怨無所集。今王方眩於佞口，
酣於亂政。楚國之人，皆貪靳尚之貴而響隨之。大夫乃孑孑
然挈其忠信而叫譟其中，言不從，國不治，徒彰乎彼非我
是，此買仇而釣禍也。”

原曰：“吾聞君子處必孝悌，仕必忠信；得其志，雖死
猶生；不得其志，雖生猶死。”諫不止。靳尚怨之，讒於王
而逐之。原仿徨湘濱，歌吟悲傷。

宋玉復喻之曰：“始大夫孑孑然挈忠信而叫譟於群佞之
中，玉為大夫危之，而言之舊矣。大夫不能從。今胡悲耶？
豈爵祿是思，國壞是念耶？”

原曰：“非也。悲夫忠信不用，楚國不治也。”

33 Qu Yuan became immortalized as the author of "Encountering Sorrow" (*Lisao*
離騷), the long opening poem of the *Verses of Chu*. Qu Yuan was a member of the royal
family of Chu, the immense southern state of the Warring States period. In vain, he
attempted to warn King Xiang of Chu (r. 298–263 BC) about the threat posed by the
western state of Qin, who would eventually complete the unification of the Chinese
territory, destroying Chu in 223 BC. After having been slandered, Qu Yuan was banished
and committed suicide by drowning in the Miluo River.

Discourse on Song Yu

Qu Yuan served Chu as chamberlain for the three royal clans.[33] King Xiang of Chu lacked virtue. The shrewd minister Jin Shang enjoyed the king's favor, and the state of Chu was ill-governed. Qu Yuan was concerned over this, and admonished King Xiang and requested that Jin Shang be dismissed. The king would not listen, and Yuan's admonitions became extreme.

His disciple, Song Yu, stopped him, saying, "Thus is the mind of the gentleman: he cultivates himself without finding fault with others, and he conceals his own usefulness instead of shining among the crowd.[xxxviii] When the right time arrives, he responds, and when approached, he gives help. He responds according to the moment, but without scheming for himself. He gives help without being zealous about his achievements.[xxxix] For this reason, no favors become attached to him, and resentment has nowhere to pile up.[xl] The king is being deluded by a sycophant and seems drunk on his own chaotic government. The inhabitants of Chu all covet the honors bestowed upon Jin Shang and follow his example like an echo follows a sound. And you are utterly alone, brandishing your loyalty and trustworthiness, shouting in their midst. Your words find no support, the state is ill-governed, and you make it obvious that you think the others are wrong and you are right. You are just looking for enmity and disaster."

Qu Yuan said, "I have been told that a gentleman will show piety towards his parents and respectful deference towards his elder brothers, and that when a gentleman serves in office he will be loyal and trustworthy. If he realizes this aspiration, he will remain alive even when dead. If he does not realize this aspiration, he will be dead even while alive."

He continued his unceasing remonstrating. Jin Shang hated him, and spoke ill of him to the king and had him expelled. So Yuan paced the bank of the River Xiang, chanting his own sadness.

Once more Song Yu explained to him, "At first, you were utterly alone, brandishing your loyalty and trustworthiness, shouting in the midst of a crowd of sycophants. This seemed dangerous, and I told you that at the time. But you couldn't follow my advice. Why are you sad now? Could it be that you are longing for noble rank and emolument or nostalgic for the state's capital?"

"Not at all," said Yuan. "I am sad because my loyalty and trustworthiness are not put to use, and because the state of Chu is ill-governed."

玉曰：“始大夫以為死孝悌忠信也，又何悲乎？且大夫
貌容形骸，非大夫之有也。美不能醜之，醜不能美之；長不
能短，短不能長；彊壯不能尫弱之，尫弱不能彊壯之；病
不能排，死不能留。形骸似乎我者也，而我非可專一。一
身尚若此，乃欲使楚人之國由我理亂，大夫之惑亦甚矣。
夫君子寄形以處世，虛心以應物，無邪無正，無是無非，無
善無惡，無功無罪。虛乎心，雖桀紂蹻跖，非罪也。存乎
心，雖堯舜夔契，非功也。則大夫之忠信，靳尚之邪佞，孰
分其是非耶？無所分別，則忠信邪佞一也。有所分，則分者
自妄也。而大夫離真以襲妄，恃己以黜人，不待王之棄逐，
而大夫自棄矣。今求乎忠信而得乎忠信，而又悲之而不能自
止，所謂兼失其妄心者也。玉聞上達節，中守節，下失節。
夫虛其心而遠於有為者，達節也。

---

34 Jie 桀 was the proverbially bad last ruler of the Xia dynasty, traditionally mentioned in
one breath with Zhòu, the cruel last Shang king. Zhuang Jiao 莊蹻 and Robber Zhi 盜
跖 are often mentioned together as the arch villains of Chinese antiquity. Robber Zhi is
the central figure in *Zhuangzi* 29.

"You originally thought that you should die for filial piety and for loyalty and trustworthiness, so why be sad?" Yu said. "Moreover, your outward appearance and your tangible body are not your property. The beautiful cannot be made ugly, and the ugly cannot be made beautiful. What is long cannot be made short, and what is short cannot be made long. The strong cannot be made frail, and the frail cannot be made strong. Sickness cannot be expelled, and death cannot be delayed. The tangible body may seem to be ours, but it is not something we can monopolize. And if this is the case for one person, then you, Grand Master, must be very deluded indeed in your desire to order the entire state of Chu alone!ˣˡⁱ

"A gentleman dwells in the world by entrusting his outward form to it. He responds to things with a mind made empty. To him, there is no unorthodox or orthodox, no right or wrong, no good or evil, no merit or crime. To a mind made empty, even Jie, Zhou, Jiao, and Zhi are not criminals.[34] As long as something is preserved within the mind, even Yao, Shun, Kui and Qi are without merit.[35] ˣˡⁱⁱ Between your loyalty and trustworthiness and Jin Shang's perniciousness and sycophancy, who divides right from wrong? If no distinction can be made, then loyalty, trustworthiness, perniciousness, and sycophancy amount to the same. And if a distinction is made, then it means that the maker of the distinction is fooling himself. You have strayed from your true nature so as to perpetuate a falsehood, and you have used your self-confidence to dismiss others.ˣˡⁱⁱⁱ You didn't have to wait until the king discarded and expelled you; you discarded yourself! You were striving for loyalty and trustworthiness, and now you have achieved loyalty and trustworthiness, but still you feel sad and cannot stop yourself. This is called being led to error twice by a fraudulent mind. I have been told that the highest category of people thoroughly understands moral steadfastness, the middle category preserves moral steadfastness, and the lower category loses moral steadfastness.[36] Emptying one's mind and keeping purposive action at a distance is thoroughly understanding moral steadfastness.

---

35 Kui 夔 and Qi 契 are said to have been two of wise king Shun's ministers.
36 A quote from the *Zuo Tradition*, fifteenth year of Duke Cheng. See Durrant, Lee, and Schaberg 2016, 819.

存其心而分是非者，守節也。得其所分又悲而撓之者，失節
也。"

　　原不達，竟沉汨羅而死。

---

37 Through its moral relativism (the distinction between good and bad cannot be made) and
its opinion that man's life is not his own property, this chapter acts as a mouthpiece for
Zhuangzi, and even more so for *Liezi*. See, for instance, the first *Liezi* chapter (Graham
1960, 29–30), where Shun asks a minister whether one can succeed in possessing the
Way, and the minister explains that a person does not even own their own body. To this,
Master Incapable adds his stress on the necessity of a mind free of conventional ideas,
ideals, and value judgments.

　　Confucius is portrayed as someone who knew that it was impossible to alter the
world's course but kept trying to do so (see *Analects* 14.38). Qu Yuan is made a paragon
of this Confucian engagement here. From a Daoist point of view, Song Yu's advice to
Qu Yuan corresponds to an elementary form of humility, because considering oneself
as the norm is hubris, and thinking that one can singlehandedly change society is a
dangerous form of delusion.

Storing things in the mind and making distinctions between right and wrong is preserving moral steadfastness. Obtaining one's allotment yet feeling sad and frustrated because of it is losing moral steadfastness."[xliv]

Yuan did not understand this, and in the end he drowned himself in the Miluo River.[37]

商隱說

漢高帝嬖於戚姬，欲以趙王如意易太子盈，大臣不能爭。呂
后危之，謀於留侯張良。良曰：“夫有非常之人，然後成非
常之事。良聞商洛山遁者四人，曰夏黃公，甪里先生，東園
公，綺里季。上嘗召不能致。今太子實能自卑以求之，四人
且來，來而實太子，此善助也。”呂后如良計，遣呂澤
迎之。

　　四人始恥之，既而相謂曰：“劉季大度，又知所以高我，
求我不得，憗己而已矣。呂雉女子，性復慘忍，其子盈不
立，必迫於危。危而求我，安危卜於我也。求我不得，必加
禍於我，姑俞之可也。”乃來。

　　一日偕太子進。高祖見而問之，四人咸自名。帝愕然
曰：“吾嘗求之而不從吾，何謂從太子？”

38 Emperor Gaozu (r. 202–195 BC), whose real name was Liu Bang 劉邦, polite name Ji
    季, was the founder of the Han dynasty. He married the daughter of Lü Wen 呂文, who
    bore him a son, Liu Ying 劉盈. The emperor, however, considered the heir-designate
    a weakling and hoped to replace him with Liu Ruyi 劉如意, the son he had with his
    concubine Qi 戚姬. Zhang Liang 張良 (262–189 BC) is considered one of the ablest
    strategists in all of Chinese history. Having assisted Liu Bang in overthrowing the Qin
    and establishing the Han, he was ennobled as the Marquis of Liu 留侯.

Discourse on the Hermits of Shang

Emperor Gao of the Han had a special fondness for Concubine Qi and wanted to replace Ying, the Grand Heir, with Ruyi, the Prince of Zhao. His highest ministers were unable to advise against it. Empress Lü considered this a perilous situation and took counsel with Zhang Liang, the Marquis of Liu.[38]

Liang said, "Only when you have extraordinary people can extraordinary feats be accomplished.[xlv] I was told that four men live in seclusion in the Shangluo mountains: Sir Huang of Xia, Master Luli, Sir Dongyuan and Qili Ji.[39] The emperor once tried to invite them here but was unsuccessful. If the Grand Heir were truly able to humble himself and entreat them now, and the four men came as guests of the Grand Heir, that would be a great help." Empress Lü did as Liang advised and dispatched Lü Ze to welcome them.[40]

At first, the four men felt disgraced by this, but soon they discussed it among themselves. "Liu Ji is magnanimous, and he understands why we should be held in high regard. When he invited us in vain, he felt ashamed. Lü Zhi is a woman, whose nature is heartless and cruel.[41] If her son Ying is not installed as emperor, she will find herself in a hazardous position. Imperiled, she seeks us out, so her safety or peril will be decided by us. If her efforts to invite us fail, she will certainly bring disaster upon us. We should say yes." And so they went to the capital.

One day, they accompanied the Grand Heir into the palace. Gaozu saw them and inquired about them, whereupon they introduced themselves. Astonished, the emperor said, "I once invited you here, but you did not agree. Why did you agree for the Grand Heir?"

---

39 Together they are known as the "four hoaryheads."

40 Lü Ze is Empress Lü's older brother.

41 One of the demonstrations of Lü Zhi's cruelty was after Emperor Gaozu's death, when the Empress had Ruyi poisoned and his mother tortured to death. Concubine Qi's hands and feet were hacked off, her eyes were gouged out and her ears burnt off, and she was left to die in a latrine, while she was referred to as the "human pig." The new emperor, Lü Zhi's son, who had attempted in vain to protect Ruyi, was so shocked by all this that he refused to play an active role in politics, allowing his mother to dominate court politics until her death in 180 BC.

　　四人曰："陛下慢人，我義不受辱。太子尊人，我即以
賓游。"帝謝之，指謂戚姬曰："太子羽翼成矣，不可搖也。"

　　呂后德之，將尊爵之。四人相謂曰："我之來，遠禍也，
非欲於心也。盈立則如意黜，呂雉得志則戚姬死。今我懼
禍，成盈而敗如意，歡呂後而愁戚姬，所謂廢人而全己，殆
非殺身成仁者也。復將忍恥，爵於女子之手，以立於廷，何
異賊人夕入人室，得金而矜富者耶？"乃復隱商山。呂後不
能留。

　　張良亦悟，於是屏氣絕穀而退居爾。

42　The "wings" (*yi* 翼) here have the meaning of "helpers" or "assistants."

43　A reference to *Analects* 15.9, where Confucius states that a person of great ambition and a
　　humane person will never try to stay alive if that harms humaneness, and will sometimes
　　even cause their own deaths in bringing about humaneness.

44　Breathing exercises and abstaining from cereals and other traditional foods are among
　　the oldest Daoist longevity practices.

The four men said, "Your majesty treated others with arrogance, and our honor does not allow us to be humiliated. The Grand Heir respects others, and so we accompany him as his guests." The emperor bade them farewell. Then he said to Concubine Qi as he pointed at the four men, "The Grand Heir's wings have grown![42] He can no longer be swayed."

Empress Lü treated the four hermits kindly and intended to honor them with noble rank. The four men discussed among themselves. "We came here to keep disaster at bay, not out of our own desire. If Ying is installed, Ruyi will be gotten rid of. If Lü Zhi realizes her ambition, Concubine Qi will die. Now, out of fear of disaster, we have brought success to Ying and failure to Ruyi. We have brought enjoyment to Empress Lü and sadness to Concubine Qi. This is called destroying others so as to keep oneself intact. We are not people who sacrifice themselves so as to achieve humaneness.[43] If we endure the shame and accept a noble rank from a woman, thus establishing ourselves at court, then how are we any different from thieves who enter people's house at night, take their gold and brag about being rich?" Thereupon they went back to their reclusive life at Mount Shang.[xlvi] Empress Lü was unable to detain them.

Zhang Liang also came to a realization, and went to live in retirement, controlling his breath and renouncing the eating of grains.[44] [xlvii]

嚴陵說

光武微時，與嚴陵為布衣之交。及即位，而陵方釣於富春渚。光武思其舊，慕其賢，躬往聘之。陵不從。

　　光武曰：“吾與子交也，今吾貴為天子，而子猶漁，吾為子恥之。吾有官爵，可以貴子，金玉可以富子，使子在千萬人上。舉動可以移山嶽，叱咤可以興雲雨，榮宗華族，聯公繼侯，丹雘宮室，雜沓車馬，美衣服，珍飲食，擊鐘鼓，合歌舞，身樂於一世，名傳於萬祀。豈與垂餌終日，泊沒無聞，校其升沉榮辱哉？可為從於我也。”

　　陵笑曰：“始吾交子之日，而子修志意，樂貧賤，似有可取者。今乃誇咤眩惑，妄人也。夫四海之內，自古以為至廣大也。十分之中，

45 Commoners wear plain garb, as opposed to silk robes. Liu Xiu 劉秀 (6 BC–57 CE) was
a scion of the Han imperial clan. In 9 CE Wang Mang 王莽 temporarily ended the Han
dynasty, establishing his own Xin 新 (“New”) dynasty. After the Xin became defunct,
Liu Xiu ruled under the name Emperor Guangwu 光武帝 (the Shining Martial Emperor)
from 25 CE until his death. Liu Xiu grew up in modest circumstances and once studied

Discourse on Yan Ling

Back when Emperor Guangwu was still living a humble life, he formed a plain-garb friendship with Yan Ling.[45] After Guangwu mounted the throne, Ling took up fishing on a sandbar in the Fuchun River. Longing for the old days, Guangwu, who admired Yan Ling's worthy character, went to pay him a visit in person.[46] Ling refused to return with him.

"We are friends," Guangwu said. "I am honored now as the Son of Heaven, but you are still a fisherman. I feel ashamed for you. I have official titles and ranks of nobility to honor you, and gold and jade to make you rich, so you may rise above the many.[xlviii] With one movement, you could shift hills and mountains, and with one shout, you could lift the clouds and rain. You would bring glory to your ancestors and splendor to your clan, and consecutive generations would be ennobled as duke or marquis. Your houses and habitations would be painted cinnabar red, and you would have many carriages and horses. You would wear beautiful clothes, and drink and eat only the finest things. Bells and drums would be struck, and songs and dances brought together. You would know joy your whole life long, and your name would be transmitted for ten thousand years. Compare that to dangling bait for the rest of your life and being buried a complete unknown. Which is higher and which lower, which is honorable and which dishonorable? You should choose to come with me."

Ling smiled and said, "When I first met you, you cultivated your ambitions, and you found happiness in poverty and a lowly status. You seemed to have something worthwhile. But now you fool others with your bragging and delusions. From of old, the territory within the four seas has been thought to be the greatest there is. Of the ten parts, half

together with the much older Yan Guang. Yan's polite name was Ziling 子陵, which is why Master Incapable calls him Yan Ling 嚴陵. When Liu Xiu mounted the throne, Yan Guang changed his name and went to live as a hermit. For a while, the new emperor managed to attract his old friend to the capital, but Yan Guang refused a court appointment and finished his days farming and fishing. See Watson 1990, 45-46.

46 In this particular context, *pin* 聘 indicates a visit, typically by sending a representative bearing gifts, to request one's presence and service at court.

山嶽江海有其半，蠻夷戎狄有其三，中國所有，一二而已。
背叛侵凌，征伐戰爭，未嘗怗息。夫中國天子之貴，在十分
天下一二分中。征伐戰爭之內，自尊者爾。夫所謂貴且尊
者，不過於一二分中，徇喜怒專生殺而已。不過一二分中，
擇土木以廣宮室，集繒帛珍寶以繁車服，殺牛羊種百穀以美
飲食，列姝麗敲金石以悅視聽而已。嗜欲未厭，老至而死，
豐肌委於螻蟻，腐骨淪於土壤，匹夫匹婦一也，天子之貴何
有哉？

　　"所謂貴我以官爵者，吾知之矣。自古帝王與公侯卿大
夫之號，皆聖人彊名，以等差貴賤而誘愚人爾。且子今之帝
王之身，昔之布衣之身也，今人雖帝子，而子自視之，何異
於昔？蓋以誘我於彊名，而使子悅而誇咤也。今又欲以彊名
公侯卿大夫誘我，非愚我耶？夫彊名者，眾人皆能為之。我
苟悅此，當自彊名曰公侯卿大夫可矣，何須子之彊名哉？子
必曰官爵者，以其富貴其身也。官爵實彊名也，自我則有富
貴之實，不自我則富貴何有哉？

47 The "central states" refers to *Zhongguo* 中國 or "China," the Middle Kingdom.

are occupied by hills, mountains, rivers, and lakes, and another three are in the possession of the southern, eastern, western, and northern barbarians. The central states own but one or two parts, where rebellions, invasions, punitive expeditions and warfare never cease.[47][xlix] The Son of Heaven of the central states is only held in esteem in one or two of the ten parts of all under heaven. In the midst of punitive expeditions and warfare, he still honors himself. However, with this so-called 'esteem' and 'honor,' he can merely preside over life and death within his one or two parts, at his own pleasure or anger. Within his parts, he selects materials to expand his palace, he collects precious items to bedeck his carriages and clothing, he kills oxen and goats and grows the manifold cereals so as to enhance his food and drink, and he lines up beautiful women and strikes clocks and chimes to please his eyes and ears, and that's about it. Before his cravings and desires have been satisfied, old age will arrive and he will die. His plump flesh will be entrusted to mole-crickets and ants, and his rotting bones will disappear into the soil, just as though he were a commoner. What is left, then, of the honor of the Son of Heaven?

"And as for what you said about honoring me with official titles and ranks of nobility, I know what that is all about! From ancient times, the appellations of 'emperor,' 'king,' 'duke,' 'marquis,' 'minister,' and 'grand master' have all been names enforced by the sages to establish a hierarchy of noble and humble, and to entice the ignorant! Moreover, you may be royal now, but you are the same person as you were back when you wore plain garb. Nowadays people may consider you 'the emperor,' but when you look at yourself, what is different from before? You are trying to entice me with enforced names, which makes you content and boastful. Do you think I am ignorant, trying to entice me today with enforced names such as 'duke,' 'marquis,' 'minister,' and 'grand master'? However you look at it, enforcing names is something everybody can do. If I enjoyed such things, I could forcibly name myself 'duke,' 'marquis,' 'minister,' or 'grand master,' and that would be fine! Why would I need you to enforce names? You will say that it is through official titles and noble ranks that a person is wealthy and honorable. In reality, however, official titles and ranks of nobility are enforced names as well. If they originate with me, then wealth and honor are a reality. If they do not, then what wealth and honor would there be?[48] Now, as far as these

---

48 Gert Naundorf has the "me" pertain to the emperor. The translation would then become: "If they originate with you [Emperor Guangwu], then wealth and honor would be a reality; if they do not originate with you, then what wealth and honor would there be?" See Naundorf 1972, 111.

夫所謂官爵富貴者，亦不過於峩冠鳴玉，驅前殿後，坐大
廈，被鮮服，耳倦絲竹，口饫椒蘭，皆子所誘我之說而已。
子所誘我者，不過充欲之物而已。夫車馬代勞也，騏驥款
段，一也。屋宇庇風雨也，丹腹蓬茅，一也。衣服蔽形也，
綺縠韋布，一也。食粒却饑也，椒蘭藜藿，一也。況吾泪乎
太虛，咀乎太和，動靜不作，陰陽同波。今方自忘其姓氏，
自委其行止，操竿投縷，泛然如寄。又何暇梏其肢體，愁其
精神，貪乎彊名，而充乎妄欲哉？

　　"且王莽更始之有天下，與子之有天下何異哉？同乎求
為中國所尊者爾，豈憂天下者耶？今子戰爭殺戮，不知紀
極，盡人之性命，得己之所欲，仁者不忍言也。而子不恥，
反以我漁為恥耶？"

　　光武慼，於是不敢臣陵焉。

49 Referring to musical instruments made of silk strings and bamboo, such as the zither
    and the flute.
50 The Great Void (*taixu* 太虛) is the total absence of distinctions; the Great Harmony
    (*taihe* 太和) indicates the harmoniously operating energies of heaven and earth.
51 Like Liu Xiu, Liu Xuan 劉玄 was a scion of the Han imperial clan. As the reign of the
    usurper Wang Mang drew to its close, Liu Xuan declared himself emperor, with Gengshi
    更始 ("Beginning Again") as his reign title. Less than two years after his bid for power,

so-called official titles, noble ranks, wealth, and honor are concerned, they do not go beyond high hats and tinkling jade, an escort in front and a guard in the rear, sitting in vast mansions, wearing brightly-colored clothes, tiring the ears with silk and bamboo, and stuffing the mouth with chilis and orchids.[49] All of this is just talk to entice me, and nothing else. And the things with which you seek to entice me do nothing more than satisfy desires. If horse and carriage are there to save labor, then a thoroughbred steed and an old nag are one and the same. If houses are there to offer protection from wind and rain, then a mansion painted cinnabar red and a weed-thatched hut are one and the same. If clothes are there to cover the body, then white silk or taffeta and tanned hides or linen are one and the same. If meals are there to drive away hunger, then spicy delicacies and goosefoot or bean leaves are one and the same.

"I am submerged in the Great Void and feed on the Great Harmony.[50] Neither movement nor stillness arise; yin and yang flow in concert. I am oblivious to my own name now and have abandoned both action and rest. Holding the fishing rod, I cast the line. The drifting life is my refuge. What time do I have to shackle my limbs and trouble my spirit to satisfy sham desires, fueled by a greed for enforced names?

"Furthermore, what difference would there be between the way Wang Mang and Gengshi took possession of all under heaven and your way?[51] You all have in common that you seek to be revered by the central states, and that you feel no concern for all under heaven! Now you wage war and you kill and slaughter without knowing where to stop. You end other people's lives to obtain what you desire. A humane person could not bear to say the things you say. And yet you feel no shame. On the contrary, you feel ashamed because I am a fisherman?"

Guangwu was embarrassed and no longer dared to regard Ling as his subject.[52][li]

the Gengshi Emperor was crushed by the Red Eyebrows, a peasant rebellion movement against Wang Mang.

52 The "real" meeting between the emperor and his old friend, as described in the chapter on recluses in the *History of the Later Han* (83.2763–2764), was rather more cordial. Yan Guang made it clear that he was not interested in an official post, but the two men, in the translation by Burton Watson (1990, 46), "lay down to sleep, and in the night Guang rested his leg on the emperor's stomach. The following day the grand historian reported that a star from another part of the sky had very suddenly invaded the constellation of the imperial throne. The emperor laughed and said, 'I was spending the night with my old friend Yan Ziling, that's all.'" When Yan Guang died, the emperor was deeply grieved and ordered local officials to present Yan's family with lavish gifts of money and grain. On Yan Guang, see also Berkowitz 2000, 103–106.

孫登說

孫登先生隱蘇門山，嵇康慕而往見之，曰：“康聞蜉蝣不能知龜齡，燕雀不能與鴻期。康之心實不足以納真誨，然而日月之照，何限乎康莊境埒；雨露之潤，罔擇乎蘭蓀蕭艾。先生理身固命之餘，願以及康，俾康超乎有涯，遨乎無垠。”

    登久而應之曰：“夫杳杳冥冥，有精非精，渾渾淳淳，有神非神。精神甚真，離之不分，留之不存。孰謂固命，孰謂理身，孰為有涯，孰為無垠？然而虛無之中，綿綿相循，出入無跡，為天地之根。知之者明，得之者尊。凡汝所論，

---

53 The Daoist master Sun Deng lived in a hole in the ground on a mountain in Henan province. In the summer he made his own clothes by weaving grass; in wintertime he let his hair hang loose to serve as a coat. He liked to read in the *Classic of Changes* and wrote a long lost commentary to the *Daodejing*. He was proficient in the Daoist technique of a sort of whistling (*xiao* 嘯), which allowed the adept to bring his own vital energies in harmony with the cosmic *qi* with a mix of vocalization, breathing technique and life prolongation. Early sources on Sun Deng recount how Ruan Ji and Xi Kang (the best-known of the Seven Sages of the Bamboo Grove 竹林七賢) visited the hermit. Ruan Ji is said to have written his famous "Biography of Master Great Man" (*Daren xiansheng zhuan* 大人先生傳) after meeting with Sun Deng. This "first declaration of utopian anarchism in Chinese history" is translated in Holzman 1976, 192-205. Xi Kang is said to have followed

Discourse on Sun Deng

Master Sun Deng lived in seclusion on Mount Sumen.[53] Xi Kang admired him and went to meet with him. He said, "I have been told that the mayfly cannot comprehend the turtle's age, and that swallows and sparrows cannot equal the swan-goose.[lii] My mind is inadequate to receive your perfect counseling. However, sunrays and moonbeams do not distinguish between spacious avenues and barren soil, and neither does the moisture of rain and dew choose between orchids and wormwood. I wish that you would share with me whatever you can spare about the ordering of the person and the consolidation of destiny, Master. Then I could transcend that which is bounded and roam where limits do not exist."

Deng took quite some time before replying, "Dark and obscure, there is an essence which is not simply 'essence.' Chaotic and uncorrupted, there is a spirit which is not simply 'spirit.'[54] Essence and spirit are the utmost Realization. You may want to separate from them, but they will not part from you. You may want to retain them, but they will not remain.[55] What, then, would you call the 'consolidation of destiny'? What would you call the 'ordering of the person'? What would be 'that which is bounded'? What would be 'where limits do not exist'? Nevertheless, amid Void and Nullity there is something that stretches on into infinity. Coming out or going in, it leaves no traces. It is the root of heaven and earth.[56] He who understands this is enlightened; he who obtains this is venerable. Everything you have discussed indicates that you have not

---

Sun Deng for three years, before receiving a rather negative appraisal from the taciturn hermit. See *Jin shu* 94.2426, Xu Zhen'e 1984, 355–356 and Mather 2002, 354–356.

54 This sentence has caused some perplexity. How can something be simultaneously "essence" and "not essence," "spirit" and "not spirit"? My interpretation goes back to the first paragraph of the *Daodejing*, where it is said that the Way that can be spoken of is not the constant Way, and the name that can be named is not the constant name. The essence and spirit Sun Deng is referring to are the "utmost Realization." They are so dark, obscure, chaotic, and uncorrupted that they cannot be simply grasped using the words "essence" and "spirit."

55 In "Illuminating the Foundation," something similar is said about "effortless action made into the center."

56 Reminiscent of *Daodejing* 6. See "True Cultivation" III.

未窺其門。吾聞諸老聃曰：良賈深藏若虛，君子盛德容貌若
愚。且夫蚌以珠剖，象以齒焚，蘭煎以膏，翠拔以文，常人
所知也。汝有藻飾之才，亡冥濛之機，如執明燭，煌煌光
輝，穹蒼所惡也。吾嘗得汝《貽山巨源絕交書》，其間二大
不可七不堪，皆矜己疵物之說，時之所憎也。夫虛其中者，
朝市不喧；欲其中者，巖谷不幽。仕不能奪汝之情，處不能
濟汝之和。仕則累，不仕則已。而又絕人之交，增以矜己疵
物之說，嘽噪於塵世之中，而欲探乎永生，可謂惡影而走於
日中者也。何足聞吾之誨哉？"

　　康眩然如醒，後果以刑死。

57　Found in Laozi's biographical sketch. See Nienhauser 1994–2019, vol. VII, 21; *Records
　　of the Historian* 63.2140.
58　Shan Juyuan 山巨源 is Shan Tao 山濤 (205–283), a friend of Xi Kang's and another of the
　　Seven Sages of the Bamboo Grove. When Shan Tao wanted to recommend Xi Kang for
　　office, an irritated Kang wrote to explain why he refused to accept an official position.
　　The letter is translated by J.R. Hightower in Birch 1965, 162–166.
59　The "seven unbearable things" are those things Xi Kang disliked about serving in an
　　official position: having to rise early, not being able to make music or go fishing when
　　one feels like it, having to wear ceremonial dress, being present at funerals, answering
　　letters, no longer being able to openly express one's thoughts, and so on.

even caught a glimpse of its gateway. From Old Longears I heard the following: 'A good tradesman hides his possessions so deep that it seems he has nothing. A gentleman of consummate virtue has an appearance of ignorance.'[57] Moreover, freshwater clams are forced open because of their pearls, elephants are burned because of their tusks, orchids are cooked to make ointment, and kingfishers have their feathers plucked to make ornaments. Any ordinary man knows this. You have a talent for literary ornamentation and embellishment, but you lack the workings of the dark and the blurry. You're like someone picking up a bright candle and spreading its dazzling glow, which the vault of heaven detests. I read your 'Letter breaking off relations with Shan Juyuan.'[58] The 'two things that are absolutely not permissible' and the 'seven unbearable things' in that letter are all self-glorification coupled with criticism of others, and your contemporaries despise you for that.[59] Someone who has made himself inwardly empty does not consider the court and market to be bustling, whereas to someone full of desires, even cliffs and valleys are not secluded. Serving in office cannot go counter to your feelings, and not having an official position cannot contribute to your inner harmony. If serving in office is troublesome, not serving is the end of all that.[liii] But you found it necessary to break off relations with someone, and to add words of self-glorification and criticism of others. Creating all this fuss in our world of dust while still wanting to explore eternal life could be described as hating shadows yet walking about in the sunshine. How could you be worthy of my teachings?"[60]

Kang looked dazed, like someone just waking up from a drunken stupor. [liv] As expected, he was later executed.[61][lv]

---

60 Sun Deng's reply to Xi Kang's flatteringly formulated question begins with an attempt to name the ineffable, incorporating a reference to *Daodejing* 6, with its "root of heaven and earth." Sun's mystical vocabulary is meant to confront Xi Kang with the latter's inability to become as dark and blurry as the Way, which every Daoist should try to embody. The hermit's reference to clams being forced open, elephants being burned, orchids being cooked, and kingfishers having their feathers plucked is an echo of *Zhuangzi*'s cult of uselessness, as put forth for example in chapter 4 with its famous statement that only worthless trees get to be old and huge. Master Incapable particularly targets Xi Kang's letter breaking off relations with Shan Tao, which is reminiscent of Song Yu's criticism of Qu Yuan.

61 Xi Kang's execution was the result of his provocative attitude towards an official who later took revenge. In "A Poem on My Indignation in Confinement" (*Youfen shi* 幽憤詩), Xi Kang admitted to being "ashamed before Sun Deng" (Owen and Swartz 2017, 293).

BOOK III

无能子卷下

答通問

无能子貧，其昆弟之子且寒而饑，嗟吟者相從焉。

一日，兄之子通謂无能子曰："嗟寒吟飢有年矣，夕則多夢祿仕，而豐乎車馬金帛；夢則樂，寤則憂，何可獲置其易哉？"

无能子曰："畫憂夕樂，均矣。何必易哉？"

通曰："夕樂夢爾。"

无能子曰："夫夢之居屋室，乘車馬，被衣服，進飲食，悅妻子，憎仇讎，憂樂喜怒，與夫寤而所欲所有為者，有所異耶？"

曰："無所異。"

"無所異，則安知寐而為之者夢耶，寤而為之者夢耶？且人生百歲，其間畫夕相半，半憂半樂，又何怨乎？夫冥乎虛而專乎常者，王侯不能為之貴，厮養不能為之賤，玉帛子女不能為之富，藜羹縕縷不能為之貧，則憂樂無所容乎其間矣。動乎情而屬乎形者，感物而已矣。物者，所謂富貴之具也。形與物，朽敗之本也，情感之而憂樂之無常也。以無常之情，縈朽敗之本，寤猶夢也，百年猶一夕也。

---

1   The name Tong means "he who comprehends."
2   Permanence (*chang* 常) is an attribute of the Way. See *Daodejing* 32: "The Way is permanent and without name" (道常無名).

Reply to Tong's Question

Master Incapable was poor. His nephews were cold and hungry, and they sighed and moaned as they followed him around.

One day Tong, the son of Master Incapable's elder brother, said to Master Incapable: "For years I've been sighing from cold and moaning from hunger! At night I often dream about having a salary and an official position, and plenty of carriages, horses, gold and silk. I'm happy when I'm dreaming and depressed when I'm awake. How can I turn that around?"[1]

Master Incapable said, "It is balanced to be depressed in the daytime and happy at night! Why would there be any need for change?"

"The happiness at night is only a dream," said Tong.

Master Incapable said, "While you dream, the house you live in, the horse and carriage you ride in, the clothes you wear, the drink and food presented to you, the wife and children you find pleasure in, the enemies you hate, the worries and happiness, the joy and anger, are they any different from what you desire and experience when awake?"

"No, there is no difference," said Tong.

"If there is no difference, then how do you know if what you do while asleep is a dream, or what you do while awake is a dream? Anyway, man lives one hundred years, of which daytime and nighttime each occupy one half. One half is spent depressed, the other happy; what is there to complain about? Someone who has immersed in the Void and who concentrates on the Permanent would not feel ennobled to become a king or a marquis, nor humbled to become a servant or slave.[2] [lvi] Jade, silk, sons, and women do not make him feel rich, and goosefoot soup and tattered clothes cannot make him feel poor. This means that inside himself he has room for neither sadness nor happiness. He who is moved by the emotions and attached to the physical form is affected by material things, and that is all! Material things are the implements of so-called 'riches and honors.' The physical form and material things are the root of decay and decline. They affect you emotionally, and you experience the impermanence of depression and happiness. If you entwine the root of decay and decline with impermanent emotions, then waking is like dreaming, and one hundred years are like a single night. If you are able

汝能冥乎虛而專乎常，則不知所以飢寒富貴矣；動乎情而屬
乎形，則晝夕痁寐俱夢矣。汝其思之！"

---

3   The influence of the third *Liezi* chapter, which demonstrates that what we call "reality"
     and "illusion" are of equal value, is unmistakable. Master Incapable's direct inspiration
     is most probably the *Liezi* anecdote about the old servant of Mr Yin, who labors all day
     long but dreams he is the lord of the estate at night. Mr Yin, owner of a huge estate, is
     plagued by worries and dreams every night that he is a mistreated slave. See Graham
     1960, 68–69; Yang Bojun 1985, 105–106.

to immerse yourself in the Void and to concentrate on the Permanent, then hunger, cold, wealth, and honors will lose all significance to you. If, however, you are moved by the emotions and attached to the physical form, then day and night, waking and sleeping are both dreams! Think about that!"[3]

答華陽子問

无能子形骸之友華陽子，為其所知迫以仕。華陽子疑，問无
能子曰：「吾將學無心久矣，仕則違心矣，不仕則忿所知，
如何其可也？」

　　无能子曰：「無心不可學。無心非仕不仕，心疑念深，
所謂見瞽者臨穽而教之前也。夫無為者無所不為也，有為者
有所不為也。故至實合乎知常，至公近乎無為，以其本無欲
而無私也。欲於中，漁樵耕牧有心也；不欲於中，帝車侯服
無心也。故聖人宜處則處，宜行則行。理安於獨善，則許由
善卷不恥為匹夫；勢便於兼濟，則堯舜不辭為天子，其為無
心，一也。堯舜在位，不以天子之貴貴乎身，是以垂衣裳而
天下治。及朱均不肖，則以之授舜，舜授禹，

4　Quoting *Daodejing* 48.

5　"Some things will be left undone" (有所不為) is a phrase absent from the Daoist classics
　but present in the *Analects* and *Mencius*. There, however, it means something different:
　there are certain things which some men will not do.

6　"Substantiality" (*shi* 實) indicates a state of being solid and really existing. "He who
　understands the Permanent (*zhichang* 知常) is enlightened," posits *Daodejing* 16.

Reply to Huayangzi's Question

Huayangzi, Master Incapable's bodily friend, was pressed to serve in office by some acquaintances. Huayangzi had doubts and asked Master Incapable, "For a long time I have been planning to learn to be free from intentionality! If I serve in office, I will go against my convictions. If I do not serve, I will anger my acquaintances. What should I do?"

Master Incapable said, "Being free from intentionality cannot be learned. Being free from intentionality has nothing to do with serving in office or not serving in office. To have doubts in your heart and to ponder deeply is what we call 'to see a blind man at the edge of a trapfall and to advise him to keep on walking.' Taking no purposive action implies that nothing will be left undone.[4] Taking action, on the other hand, implies that some things will be left undone.[5] The reason ultimate substantiality fits with an understanding of the Permanent and ultimate impartiality comes close to nonpurposive action is that they are fundamentally free of desire and self-interest.[6] If you have desire within you, then even as a fisherman, a firewood gatherer, a farmer, or a shepherd, you will have intentionality. If you have no desire within you, then even as an emperor in his carriage or a nobleman in his robes, you will be free of intentionality. Therefore the sage will stay secluded when it is proper to stay secluded, and will act when it is proper to act. Because it was the principle of Xu You and Shanjuan to find peace in isolated self-improvement, they were not ashamed to remain commoners.[7] Because it could bring universal benefit, neither Yao nor Shun refused to become Son of Heaven. In being free of intentionality, they were all one. When Yao and Shun were on the throne, they did not honor themselves with the honor shown to a Son of Heaven. They let their robes hang down and the empire was well-ordered.[8] When Danzhu and Shangjun proved unworthy, Yao handed over the throne to Shun, and Shun handed over

---

7   Shanjuan ("he who is good at rolling himself up") is a legendary recluse mentioned in *Zhuangzi* 28 and *juan* 1 of *Lives of Eminent Gentlemen*. Shun offered the throne to Shanjuan, who refused because of his unfettered lifestyle and his contentment with living in harmony with nature.

8   The *Xici* commentary to the *Classic of Changes* says the Yellow Emperor, Yao, and Shun are said to have "let their robes hang down and the empire was well-ordered" (垂衣裳而天下治).

捨其子如疣贅，去天下如涕唾，是以歷萬祀而天下思。周
公，文王之子，武王之弟，天下熟其德矣，以成王在，其勢
不便於己，故不為天子。以成王幼，其勢宜於居攝，故不敢
辭。是以全周之祀，活周之民，巍巍成功，其德不虧，此皆
不欲於中，而無所不為也。子能達此，雖鬥雞走狗於屠肆之
中，搴旗斬將於兵陣之間，可矣，況仕乎？"

9   Danzhu 丹朱 was the son of Yao; Shangjun 商均 was Shun's son. According to tradition,
     both sons were unworthy of their father, which is why Yao and Shun ceded the throne to
     a nonrelative. Master Incapable's contemporary Luo Yin devoted an essay to Danzhu and
     Shangjun, claiming that their incompetence was not a decisive factor: even if they had
     been worthy successors, their respective fathers would still have chosen an outsider for
     the throne, in order to show that impartiality is to be preferred over descent, and thus
     over the formation of a dynasty. See De Meyer 1996, 82. Yu is the legendary founder of
     the Xia dynasty.

the throne to Yu.[9] Each excluded his own son as if he were a wart or a tumor, and let go of the empire as if it were snot or spit. Because of this, the empire will think of them with affection even after ten thousand years. The Duke of Zhou was King Wen's son and King Wu's younger brother, and the empire knew his virtue well. With King Cheng on the throne, circumstances were unfavorable for him, so he did not become a Son of Heaven.[10] Because King Cheng was still a child, it was suitable for him to act as regent, and he dared not refuse. Thus he kept the sacrifices of the Zhou intact, and kept the people of the Zhou alive.[11] His achievements were lofty, and his virtue never diminished. All of this illustrates that with freedom from inner desires nothing will be left undone. If you can understand that, then you may even engage in cock fighting and dog racing in the butcher's market, or to pick up the enemy's flag and behead the enemy general on the battlefield, not to mention serve in office!"[12]

10 King Cheng 成王 ruled over the Zhou in the second half of the eleventh century BC. His uncle, the Duke of Zhou, is widely regarded as an able and loyal regent, and he is credited with the authorship of part of the *Classic of Changes* as well as with the creation of the theory of the Heavenly Mandate.

11 "Keeping the sacrifices intact" (*quansi* 全祀) means ensuring their continuity.

12 Once more, Master Incapable illustrates the importance of being free of intentionality. One can do anything, provided one is free of desire and free of intentionality. As in the case of Lü Wang and the Count of the West ("Discourse on King Wen"), Master Incapable is remarkably mild in his judgment of historical figures universally praised in the Confucian tradition, most notably the Duke of Zhou, and his "anarchism" is miles away.

答愚中子問

无能子心友愚中子病心，祈藥於无能子。

　　无能子曰："病何？"

　　曰："痛。"

　　曰："痛在何？"

　　曰："在心。"

　　曰："心在何？"

　　愚中子告病已間矣。

　　无能子曰："此人可謂得天之真，而神光不昧者也。"

13　Nowhere is Master Incapable's ideal of being free of intentionality stated more succinctly,
　　or some would say more *koan*-like, than here. Yuzhongzi—it is no accident that his name
　　means "Master in ignorance"—has suddenly reached the insight that it is impossible
　　to suffer from a heart-mind that is simply not there. Note that the aim and the means
　　coincide, for it is by becoming free of "mind" or intentionality that one realizes freedom
　　from "mind" or intentionality. If Master Incapable comes very close to Chan Buddhism,
　　it is in this short chapter.

Reply to Yuzhongzi's Question

Master Incapable's bosom friend Yuzhongzi suffered in his heart-mind and asked Master Incapable for a remedy.

Master Incapable said, "What kind of ailment is it?"

"It hurts."

"Where does it hurt?"

"In my heart-mind."

"Where is the heart-mind situated?"

At that, Yuzhongzi announced that he was cured.

Master Incapable said, "It may be said of this man that he has obtained natural perfection, and that his spiritual glow will not be obscured."[13]

魚說

河有龍門，隸古晉地，禹所鑿也。懸水數十仞，淙其聲。雷
然一舍之間，河之巨魚，春則連群集其下，力而上泝，越其
門者則化為龍，於是挐雲拽雨焉。河墟纖鱗望之，相謂曰：
"彼亦魚也，而超變如此，豈與我撥撥然墟而游，戢戢然穴
而藏哉？"

　　其一曰："惑矣！汝之思也。夫天地之內，物之頒形者
千萬焉，形之巨細，分之大小相副焉。隨其形，足其分，各
適矣。彼超變者，河之時波則與之驚，澄則與之平，意順力
渾，沉浮安定。及其思變也，連群而妬，泝瀑而怒，意撓力
困，乃雲乃雨。夫雲雨來隨蒸潤之氣，自相感爾，於彼何有
哉？彼若有心於雲雨之間，有時而墮矣。無心自感，又何功
乎？角其上，足其下，與吾鬐鬛一也。吾鬐鬛而游，彼角足
而騰，未嘗不順也。豈以吾墟游之無爭，穴藏之無虞，人不
知而害不加之樂，易其角足雲雨之勞乎？"

14　This Dragon Gate (Longmen 龍門) is not to be confused with the Buddhist Longmen
　　cave complex south of Luoyang. Situated on the border of Shaanxi and Shanxi provinces,
　　not far from where Master Incapable lived in 887, it marks a strait in the Yellow River.

Discourse on Fish

On the Yellow River, there is a Dragon Gate carved out by Yu in the territory of the old state of Jin.[14] The water crashes down a height of more than one hundred feet, and even a day's march away it still sounds like thunder. In spring, the biggest fish in the river form schools and assemble at the foot of Dragon Gate, swimming against the current with all their might. Those who go beyond the gate are transformed into dragons, who thereupon seize the clouds and attract the rain.

Some small fish close to the riverside observed this and said to each other, "They're fish too, but what a transformation they undergo after their leap! Why would they splash around with us by the riverbank, or form huge shoals and hide in cavities?"

One of them said, "Don't be foolish! However you look at it, the things between heaven and earth take on a huge variety of shapes. The size of the outward form matches the importance of one's allotment. Everyone is comfortable when one acts in accordance with one's outward form and finds satisfaction in one's allotment. As far as those who leap and transform are concerned, when the river is turbulent, they get excited, and when the river is clear and calm, they become tranquil. Their frame of mind is one of compliance, and their strength is undivided. Whether diving or floating, they feel safe. When they think of their transformation, they form schools and become jealous. Swimming upstream, they become furious. They exhaust their strength in their aggravation.[lvii] With that, clouds rise up and it rains.

"Now, clouds and rain are the result of moist vapors rising and influencing each other. What do fish and dragons have to do with it? If they were to have intentions between the clouds and the rain, then they would frequently fall![lviii] But as this is all about spontaneous influence, without intentionality, what would the dragons have achieved? They have horns on top and legs underneath, which is exactly like us having dorsal fins and a barbel. We swim with our dorsal fins and barbel, they soar with their horns and legs, and this has never been disagreeable. Our quarrel-free life swimming by the banks, our freedom from worries while hiding in cavities, the happiness we derive from not being known to man, so that he cannot harm us—why would we exchange all that for their struggles with horns, legs, clouds, and rain?"[lix]

鴆說

鴆與蛇相遇，鴆前而啄之。

　　蛇謂曰：“世人皆毒子矣。毒者，惡名也。子所以有惡名者，以食我也。子不食我則無毒，不毒則惡名亡矣。”

　　鴆笑曰：“汝豈不毒於世人哉？指我為毒，是欺也。夫汝毒於世人者，有心嚙人也。吾怨汝之嚙人，所以食汝示刑也。世人審吾之能刑汝，故畜吾以防汝。又審汝之毒染吾毛羽肢體，故用殺人。吾之毒，汝之毒也。吾疾惡而蒙其名爾。然殺人者，人也。猶人持兵而殺人也，兵罪乎，人罪乎？則非吾之毒也，明矣。世人所以畜吾而不畜汝又明矣。吾無心毒人，而疾惡得名，為人所用，吾所為能後其身也，後身而甘惡名，非惡名矣。汝以有心之毒，盱睢於草莽之間，伺人以自快。今遇我，天也，而欲詭辯苟免耶？”

　　蛇不能答。鴆食之。

　　夫昆蟲不可以有心，況人乎？

15　Long thought to have been a fabulous creature, the poison bird (*zhen* 鴆) has been variously identified as the *pitohui dichrous* or, more probably, the crested serpent eagle (*spilornis cheela*). It is mentioned in the *Classic of Mountains and Seas* (*Shanhai jing* 山海經), and Guo Pu's 郭璞 third-century commentary to it describes it as being the size of a buzzard, with a purple belly, green feathers, a long neck, and a red beak. See Yuan Ke 1983, 152. According to tradition, it fed on poisonous snakes, as a result of which its feathers, meat, and excrement became poisonous. The poisonous feathers are said to have been steeped in wine and used in assassinations.

Discourse on the Poison Bird

A poison bird met with a snake, moved towards it and pecked at it.[15]

The snake said, "Everyone considers you poisonous! To be considered poisonous is an evil reputation. The reason you have this evil reputation is that you eat us. If you didn't eat us, you wouldn't be poisonous, and if you weren't poisonous, your bad reputation would vanish!"

The poison bird smiled and said, "Do you really mean to say that you are not poisonous to humans? Yet you point at me for being poisonous, which is a farce. You are poisonous to humans because you have the intention of biting people. I hate that you bite people, so I punish you by eating you. The people of the world know perfectly well that I am able to punish you, and therefore they nourish me as a defense against you. They also understand that your poison infects my plumage, limbs, and body, and that's why they use them to kill others. My poison is your poison. I am hostile to evil, yet I have an evil reputation. But it is people who kill other people. It's like when someone takes a weapon and kills someone: who is to blame, the weapon or the man? That makes it clear that I'm not the one doing the poisoning! And it is also clear why people nourish us and not you! I don't have the intention to poison people, but I am hostile to evil, and from that I obtain my reputation.[lx] I'm used by people, and I can put myself last in whatever I do.[lxi] Putting myself last, I willingly bear my evil reputation, and so it is no longer an evil reputation! You, however, with the poison of intentionality, lie wide-eyed in the undergrowth, and spy on people for your own amusement. That you have encountered me today is natural, and yet you would like to worm your way out by using a deceitful argument?"

The snake was unable to come up with an answer, and the poison bird ate it.

Now, if even creeping animals cannot afford to have intentionality, how much less can people?

答魯問

一

无能子從父之弟魯，求學於无能子。

无能子曰："何學？"

曰："學行學文。"

无能子曰："吾不知所以行，所以文，然前志中所謂聖人者，吾嘗偶觀之。其言曰：行，行也，行其心之所善也。文，儀也，飾其所行之善也。喪者本乎哀。哀，行也；齊縗之服，祭祀之具，文也。禮者本乎敬。敬，行也；升降揖讓，文也。樂者本乎和。和，行也；陶匏絲竹，文也。文出於行，行出於心，心出於自然。不自然則心生，心生則行薄，行薄則文縟，文縟則偽，偽則亂，亂則聖人所以不能救也。夫總其根者不求其末，專其源者不尋其流，汝能證以無心，還其自然，前無聖人，上無玄天，行與文在乎無學之中矣。"

16 Lu 魯, the name of the state where Confucius was born, means "slow-witted," "stupid," or "backward." It is probably no coincidence that Master Incapable has chosen this name for his younger uncle, as the content here is also in the *Analects*, where the four topics taught by Confucius are enumerated: "The Master based his teaching on four things: refinement (or culture, *wen* 文), the right conduct, loyalty, and trustworthiness" (see *Analects* 7.25).

17 Once more, as in the "Reply to Huayangzi's Question," we are told that certain things cannot be studied. In the reply to Huayangzi, it was being free of intentionality; here it is the right conduct and refinement. The reason why these "disciplines" cannot or need not be studied is that the right course of action or demeanor will automatically reveal itself to those who are free of intentionality and to those who return to what-is-so-of-itself. "Before you there have never been any sages, above you there is no mysterious heaven": here Master Incapable comes very close to the anarchist *Ni Dieu ni maître*.

Reply to Lu's Questions

I

Lu, a younger brother of Master Incapable's uncle, sought to receive Master Incapable's teaching.[16]

Master Incapable said, "What do you want to study?"

"I would like to study the right conduct and refinement."

"I don't know whereby one adopts the right conduct or becomes refined," Master Incapable said. "But I once happened to observe those called 'sages' in earlier treatises.[lxii] They said the following. The right conduct means 'to put into practice,' and more specifically, to put into practice what the mind holds to be good. Refinement refers to one's demeanor; it is an embellishment of the good that one practices. Mourning has its foundation in the sorrow of losing a loved one. Feeling sorrowful is the right conduct, and the mourning garb hemmed with rough hemp and the objects for the ceremonial sacrifice are the refinement.[lxiii] The rites have their foundation in respect. Respect is the right conduct, and the rising and descending, saluting with the hands joined at the chest, and a deferential attitude are the refinement. Music has its foundation in harmony. Harmony is the right conduct, and the musical instruments made of pottery, calabash, silk, or bamboo are refinements. Refinement comes from the right conduct, the right conduct comes from the mind, and the mind comes from what-is-so-of-itself. When the what-is-so-of-itself is lacking, the mind becomes active, and when the mind becomes active, then the right conduct is depleted. When the right conduct is depleted, the refinement becomes extravagant, and when the refinement is extravagant, it leads to artificiality. From artificiality comes disorder, and disorder is the reason the sages are unable to bring succor.

"Those who hold fast to the root do not seek what is non-essential, and those who concentrate on the source do not search out tributaries. If you are able to ascertain this by being free of intentionality, and you return to what-is-so-of-itself, then before you there have never been any sages, above you there is no mysterious heaven, and the right conduct and refinement are found where there is nothing to be studied."[17]

二

魯他日又問曰：“魯嘗念未得而憂，追已往而悲，得酒酣醉，陶然不知，今則不能忘乎酒矣。”

无能子曰：“汝之憂，汝之悲，自形乎？自心乎？”

曰：“自心。”

曰：“心可覷乎？”

曰：“不可覷。”

无能子曰：“不可覷者，憂悲之所生也。求憂悲之所生，且不可覷，憂悲何寄哉？憂悲無寄，則使汝遂其未得，還其已往，又將誰付耶？今汝隨而悲憂之，是欲繫風擒影也。汝無憂悲之所寄，而有味酒之陶然，不能自得，反浸漬於麴蘖，豈釀器乎？”

II

On another occasion, Lu asked, "I've been thinking about all the things I have not yet realized, and it makes me worry. I felt sad thinking of the past, so I got drunk on wine and felt contented and unknowing. But now I can't forget about the wine!"

Master Incapable said, "Do your worries and sadness come from your body? Or do they come from your mind?"

"They come from my mind."

"Can you see your mind?"

"No, I can't."

"It is from something invisible that your worries and sadness arise," Master Incapable said. "If you look for the source of your worries and sadness, and it turns out to be invisible, where would your worries and sadness lodge? If they have no place to lodge, that enables you to pursue what you have not yet realized, and to look back on time past, without becoming dependent on anything at all![lxiv] Now you are indolent but still sad and worried, and that is like wanting to truss up the wind or to catch shadows.[lxv] You don't have a place for your worries and sadness to lodge, but you do have the pleasure you derive from delicious wine. Unable to find satisfaction within yourself, you steep yourself in alcohol. What are you, some kind of vessel for brewing?"[lxvi]

紀見

一

秦市幻人，有能烈鑊膏而溺其手足者，烈鑊不能壞，而幻人
笑容焉。无能子召而問之。

幻人曰："受術於師，術能却火之熱。然而訣曰，視鑊
之烈，其心先忘其身。手足枯枿也，既忘枯枿手足，然後術
從之。悸則術敗。此吾所以得之。"

无能子顧謂其徒曰："小子志之。無心於身，幻人可以
寒烈鑊，況上德乎？"

二

无能子寓於秦村景氏民舍，一夕梟鳴其樹，景氏色憂，將彈
之，无能子止之。

景氏曰："梟，凶鳥也。人家將兇則梟來鳴，殺之則庶
幾無凶。"

无能子曰："人之家因其鳴而凶，梟罪也。梟可凶人，
殺之亦不能弭其已凶。將凶而鳴，非梟忠而先示於人耶？凶
不自梟，殺之害忠也。

---

18 Wang Ming believes Qin 秦 to be short for Da Qin, or the Roman Empire, and quotes a
remark in the third-century *Wei lüe* 魏略 saying that there were many illusionists in Da
Qin. Qin more likely refers to the "Qin village" in the first line of the next section. See
Wang Ming 1981, 43. See also Stein 1963, 8–21, for a discussion of the relation between
the Daoist mass movements of the second century and the idealized kingdom of Da Qin.

Records of Things Witnessed

I

Among the illusionists in the market of Qin, there was one who could immerse his hands and feet in a heavy cauldron filled with seething oil.[18][lxvii] The searing cauldron caused him no harm; on the contrary, the illusionist maintained his smile. Master Incapable called the man over and questioned him.

The illusionist said: "I received a technique from my master, and thanks to that, I can remove the heat from the fire. There's a formula that goes like this: 'When you see the cauldron boil, your mind should first forget your body.' Your hands and feet will become like withered stumps. Once you have forgotten the withered stumps that are your hands and feet, the technique will work well. If you panic, the technique will fail. This is how I mastered it."

Master Incapable turned his head and said to his disciples: "Take note of this, my boys! With a body that has been freed of the mind, this illusionist can treat a seething cauldron as if it were cold. Imagine what the highest power might be capable of!"[lxviii]

II

Master Incapable lodged in the commonfolk house of a Mr. Jing in Qin Village.[19] One evening, an owl called from a tree. Mr. Jing looked anxious and was about to shoot the bird, but Master Incapable stopped him.

Mr. Jing said, "The owl is an inauspicious bird. When something terrible is about to happen, the owl comes and calls.[lxix] If I kill it, there's a good chance nothing terrible will befall us."

Master Incapable said, "If something terrible happens to one's family because of an owl calling, then the bird is indeed the culprit.[20] Supposing the owl is able to cause something terrible to happen to humans, killing it will not put a stop to it. But if the owl calls as the terrible thing is about to happen, is it not loyal of the owl to first announce it to people? If the terrible thing is not caused by the owl, then killing it amounts to harming

---

19 Or, "a village in Qin," as Shaanxi Province was once part of the expanding Qin state in the third century BC.

20 Or: then the bird is to be blamed.

矧自謂人者，與夫毛群羽族，俱生於天地無私之氣，橫目方足，虛飛實走，有所異者，偶隨氣之清濁厚薄，自然而形也，非宰於愛憎者也，誰令梟司其凶耶？謚梟之凶，誰所自耶？天地言之耶？梟自言之耶？天地不言，梟自不言，何為必其凶耶？謚梟之凶，不知所自，則羽儀五色，謂之鳳者未必祥，梟未必凶。"景氏止，家亦不凶。

三

樊氏之族有美男子，年三十，或被髮疾走，或終日端居不言。言則以羊為馬，以山為水。凡名一物，多失其常名。其家及鄉人狂之，而不之錄焉。无能子亦狂之。

　　或一日遇於藜蓁間，就而歎曰："壯男子也，貌復豐碩，惜哉病如是。"

　　狂者徐曰："吾無病。"

　　无能子愕然曰："冠帶不守，起居無常，失萬物之名，忘家鄉之禮，此狂也，何謂無病乎？"

　　狂者曰："被冠帶，節起居，愛家人，敬鄉里，豈我自然哉？蓋昔有妄作者，文之以為禮，使人習之至於今。而薄醨固醇酎也，

21　Master Incapable attacks superstition using materialist or naturalistic arguments, in the tradition of Wang Chong. That heaven and earth do not speak was already stated in the *Analects* (17.19) and *Mencius* (Book V, Part 1). People with horizontal eyes were thought to have been preceded by human beings with vertical eyes, who eventually became extinct. In Yi 彝 creation myths such as *Aheixinimo* 阿黑西尼摩 or *Chamu* 查姆, the transition from vertical-eyed to horizontal-eyed still occupies an important place.

loyalty. But there is more. Those who call themselves humans, along with the hairy hordes and the feathered tribes, are born from the impartial energies of heaven and earth. If there are any differences between the human beings who have horizontal eyes and squarish feet, the birds who fly in the sky, and the mammals who walk on solid ground, then these are accidental results of the *qi* being pure or turbid and generously meted out or not. They take shape in a spontaneous fashion, without being governed by love or hate. Who would have ordered that the owl has authority over ill omens? Who is responsible for the owl's reputation as an inauspicious bird? Did heaven and earth say it? Does the owl himself say it? Heaven and earth do not speak, and neither does the owl. Why, then, must he be inauspicious? Since we do not know where the owl's reputation as an inauspicious bird comes from, then the bird with the five-colored plumed ornaments we call the 'phoenix' is not necessarily a favorable omen, and owls need not be inauspicious."

Mr. Jing desisted, and no harm befell his family.[21]

III

In Mr. Fan's extended family was a handsome man of about thirty years old. Sometimes he would run around with his hair loose over his shoulders, and other times he would sit all day long without saying a word. When he did speak, he took goats to be horses, and mountains to be rivers. Whenever he named something, he would usually neglect its habitual name. His family and fellow villagers considered him crazy but took no further notice.[lxx] Master Incapable also thought him crazy.

One day Master Incapable met the man in the shade of a grove of trees. He approached him and said with a sigh, "How regretful that a man in the prime of health and with a handsome and imposing appearance has to be so stricken with illness!"[lxxi]

"I am not ill," the madman said with dignity.

Dumbfounded, Master Incapable said, "You do not hold to the cap and sash, there's no regularity to your daily life, you are not careful about the names of the myriad things, and you disregard the etiquette of your family and native region.[22] That is insanity. Why say you are not ill?"

The madman said, "Wearing the cap and sash, leading a well-regulated daily life, being attached to my family members, respecting my native place—how would that be natural to me?[lxxii] A long time ago, there must have been charlatans who civilized our spontaneous natures, creating ceremonial forms and making people practice them up to the present day. However, a weak brew is made on the basis of a strong wine.[lxxiii]

---

22 Not holding to the cap and sash means not valuing the life of officialdom.

知之而反之者，則反以為不知，又名之曰‘狂’。且萬物之
名，亦豈自然著哉？清而上者曰天，黃而下者曰地，燭畫者
曰日，燭夜者曰月；以至風雲雨露，煙霧霜雪；以至山嶽江
海，草木鳥獸；以至華夏夷狄，帝王公侯；以至士農工商，
皁隸臧獲；以至是非善惡，邪正榮辱，皆妄作者彊名之也。
人久習之，不見其彊名之初，故沿之而不敢移焉。昔妄作者
或謂清上者曰地，黃下者曰天，燭畫者月，燭夜者日，今亦
沿之矣。彊名自人也，我亦人也，彼人何以彊名，我人胡為
不可哉？則冠帶起居，吾得以隨意取舍；萬狀之物，吾得以
隨意自名。狂不狂吾且不自知，彼不知者狂之亦宜矣！”

23 The final sentence may also be translated as: "It is entirely befitting for me to consider
    the others, who are also ignorant, as insane!" Master Incapable has almost reached the
    logical endpoint of his theory of *qiangming*, the enforcing of names; almost, because in
    order to make himself understood, he is forced to utilize conventional language himself.
    Had he followed his own line of reasoning to its logical conclusion, he could have writ-
    ten a book in an entirely made-up language, or he could have resorted to the wordless
    conversation Zhuangzi dreamed about when he sighed: "Where can I find a man who
    has forgotten words so I can have a word with him" 吾安得夫忘言之人而與之言哉? See
    Watson 1968, 302. Names, and the value systems we connect to them, are arbitrary and
    have no universal validity. "Any fool can make a rule, and every fool will mind it," wrote
    Henry David Thoreau in his journal of February 3, 1860.

Those who understand this and go counter to it are thought to 'lack un-derstanding' and are called 'insane.' But more, how could the names of the myriad things have manifested themselves spontaneously? The pure thing that has risen up is called 'heaven,' the yellow thing that has come down is called 'earth,' the thing that shines during daytime is called 'sun,' and the thing that shines at night is called 'moon.' As to wind and clouds, rain and dew, mist and fog, frost and snow, hills and peaks, rivers and seas, plants and trees, birds and beasts, the Chinese and the Barbari-ans, emperors and kings, dukes and marquises, gentlemen and peasants, artisans and merchants, menials and servitors, male and female slaves, right and wrong, good and bad, unorthodox and orthodox, honor and dishonor: these are all names enforced by charlatans. People have been repeating them for so long that they have lost sight of the fact that they were enforced names from the very beginning. Therefore they go along with them and dare not make any alterations. Suppose the charlatans of long ago had named the pure thing that has risen up 'earth,' and the yellow thing that has come down 'heaven,' and suppose they had called the thing that shines during daytime 'moon,' and the thing that shines at night 'sun.' People nowadays would still go along with it! The enforcing of names comes from humans. I am a human too. Why are other people allowed to enforce names, but I am not? So it is up to me to accept or reject the cap and sash and a well-regulated daily life. It is up to me to decide which names I apply to the things in their endless variety. Whether I am insane or not is something I myself do not know. That the others, who do not know either, consider me insane, is therefore entirely befitting!"[23] [lxxiv]

固本

一

五兵者，殺人者也。羅網者，獲鳥獸蟲魚者也。聖人造之，
然後人能相殺，而又能取鳥獸魚蟲焉。使之知可殺，知可
取，然後制殺人之罪，設山澤之禁焉。及其衰世，人不能保
父子兄弟，鳥獸魚蟲不暇育麛鹿鯤鮞，法令滋彰而不可禁，
五兵羅網教之也。造之者復出，其能自已乎？

二

棺槨者，濟死甚矣。然其工之心，非樂於濟彼也，迫於利
也。欲其日售則幸死，幸死非怨於彼也，迫於利也。醫者樂
病，幸其必瘳，非樂於救彼而又德彼也，迫於利也。棺槨與
醫，皆有濟救，幸死幸生之心，非有憎愛，各諧其所欲爾。

---

24 The wording is somewhat unclear here, indicating either the crime of killing a human,
    or those crimes that are punishable by death. These interdictions disallow hunting and
    fishing in spring.
25 An alternative translation for *jiao* 教 would be "brought that about."

Consolidating the Foundation

I

The five weapons are used to kill people. Nets are used to catch birds, wild animals, insects, and fish. They were fashioned by the sages, and since then humans have been able to kill each other, as well as capture birds, wild animals, fish, and insects. The sages made it known to man that it was permissible to kill and to capture. After that, they announced the regulations concerning the crime of killing other people and established the interdictions concerning mountains and marshes.[24]

In our age of decadence, in which a man is unable to protect his own father, son, or brother, and in which birds, wild animals, fish, and insects lack the time to nurture their fawns and roe, laws and commands are increasingly displayed, but they do not prohibit anything.[lxxv] The five weapons and the nets taught us that.[25] If those who fashioned them were to emerge once more, would they be able to stop themselves?[26]

II

Coffins are immensely helpful to the dead, but the mind of the artisan who makes the coffins does not derive pleasure from helping others. He is compelled by profit. Because he wants to sell coffins every day, he hopes that people will die. But the fact that he hopes that people will die does not mean that he hates others. He is compelled by profit.

A doctor takes pleasure in sick people. That he hopes they will recover does not mean that he shows them kindness because he derives pleasure from saving them. He is compelled by profit.

Coffins and doctors are both helpful, but in the minds of those who hope that people will die and of those who hope that people will live there is neither hate nor love: each of them accords with his own wishes.

---

26 Master Incapable quotes *Daodejing* 57, which warns against the proliferation of laws and regulations. The impossibility of making people respect the laws is treated in *Zhuangzi* 10 (see Watson 1968, 110). The theme of animals lacking the time to nurture their offspring is also addressed in the poem "Fisherman on a Southern Stream" (*Nanjing yufu* 南涇漁父) by Lu Guimeng, whose *Songling ji* (compiled with Pi Rixiu) helped preserve some of the poems by putative *Master Incapable* author Zhang Bi. See Liu and Lo 1975, 255–256.

故無為之仁天下也，無棺槨與醫之利，在其濟死瘳病之間而
已。

三

角觸蹄踏，蛇首蝎尾，皆用其所長也。審其所用，故得防其
所用而制之。是以所用長者，不如無用。食桑之蟲，絲其腸
者曰蠶，以絲自舍曰繭；繭伏而化，於是羽而蛾焉。其稟也
宜如此，猶獸之胎，鳥之卵，俱非我由也。智者知其絲可
縷，縷可織，於是烹而縷之，機杼以織之，幅而繒之，繒而
衣之。

　　夫蠶自繭將為蛾也，非為乎人謀其衣而甘乎烹也。所以
烹者，絲所累爾。烹之者，又非疾其蠶也，利所繫爾。夫獸
之胎，鳥之卵，蠶之繭，俱其所稟也。蠶所稟獨乎絲，絲必
烹，似乎不幸也，不幸似乎分也。故無為者，無幸無不幸，
何分乎？

四

有為，善不必福，惡不必禍，或制於分焉。故聖人貴乎無
為。坯蟻井蛙，示以虎豹之山、鯨鯢之海，必疑，熟其所見
也。

---

27 Master Incapable's argument builds on the conclusion of the previous chapter: for some-
    one who understands nonpurposive action, luck and allotment play no meaningful role.
    And thus Master Incapable shifts his attention to purposive action, before concluding
    with a return to nonpurposive action and an exhortation to break with custom. We
    may notice the influence of the *Balanced Discourses* (*Lunheng* 論衡), which repeatedly
    expresses that good does not necessarily lead to good fortune and evil not necessarily
    to disaster. See Forke 1907, Part I, 139, 156 and Part II, 15; Beijing daxue lishixi 1979, 81,
    335, 1023.

Therefore, when nonpurposive action treats all under heaven with humaneness, it does so without the profit-seeking of the coffin-maker and the doctor. It is situated somewhere between helping the dead and curing the sick.[lxxvi]

III

Animals with horns butt, animals with hooves stamp; snakes use their heads, scorpions their tails. All make use of their own strong point. If you closely examine what they utilize, you can defend yourself against it, and thereby control them. Therefore, it is better not to use your own strong point than to use it.

The insect that feeds on mulberry leaves and whose intestines produce silk is called the silkworm. The dwelling it makes with its own silk is called a cocoon. Hidden in its cocoon, the silkworm undergoes a transformation, whereupon it grows wings and becomes a moth. These are its natural qualities, and they are what is proper to it, in the same way that mammals have wombs and birds lay eggs. None of them acts on its own initiative. Knowledgeable people understand that silk can be made into fibers and the fibers can be used to weave cloth. So they boil the cocoons and make fibers out of them, which they weave with looms. The widths of silk are made into silk fabrics, and the silk fabrics into clothes.

Now, the silkworm makes its own cocoon in order to become a moth.[lxxvii] It does not enjoy being boiled because man intends to make clothes out of it. It gets boiled because it is has become "tied up" with the silk. Similarly, the person who boils the cocoon does not do so because he hates the silk-worm: he is "bound" by profit.

The womb of mammals, the eggs of birds, and the cocoon of silkworms are all things with which they have been naturally endowed. That only the silkworm is naturally endowed with silk and that because of the silk he will definitely be boiled is seemingly bad luck, and bad luck is seemingly one's allotment. In the case of nonpurposive action, there is no good luck nor bad luck, so what does allotment have to do with it?[lxxviii]

IV

In the case of purposive action, doing good does not necessarily lead to good fortune, and evil does not necessarily lead to disaster, as if they were controlled by allotment. Therefore the sage esteems nonpurposive action.[27]

When you show a mountain with tigers and leopards or a sea with whales to an ant in an anthill, or to a frog in a well, they will certainly grow suspicious: they are only familiar with what they themselves have

嗜欲世務之人，語以無為之理，必惑，宿於所習也。於是父
不能傳其子，兄不能傳其弟，沉迷嗜欲，以至於死，還其元
而無所生者，舉世無一人焉。

　嗟乎！無為在我也，嗜欲在我也，無為則靜，嗜欲則
作，靜則樂，作則憂。常人惑而終不可使之達者，所習藏之
也，明者背習焉。

28　The image of the frog in the well, with whom one cannot talk about the sea because he
　　is confined to the limits of the hole where he lives, comes from *Zhuangzi* 17. See Watson
　　1968, 186; Guo Qingfan 1985, 598.

seen.[28] When you talk about the principle of nonpurposive action to people who crave and desire worldly pursuits, they will certainly feel puzzled: they dwell in what they are habituated to. And thus fathers are unable to pass it on to their sons, and elder brothers are unable to pass it on to their younger brothers.[29] They are lost in cravings and desires until death. In the whole world there is not a single person who returns to the origin and does not allow any cravings and desires to arise.

So! Nonpurposive action is our own choice, and cravings and desires are our own choice. Nonpurposive action leads to serenity, while cravings and desires lead to undertakings. Serenity leads to happiness, and undertakings lead to worrying. That ordinary humans are deluded and can never be made to attain insight means that their customs are an obstruction to them.[30] Those who are enlightened turn their back on custom.

---

29 The same theme is treated in *Zhuangzi* 29 about Robber Zhi, see Watson 1968, 323; Guo Qingfan 1985, 991.

30 *Zheng* 癥, normally indicating intestinal obstruction.

Endnotes

Text-critical Endnotes to Book I

i. The "undivided life-force of Chaos" (*hundun yiqi*) indicates the undifferentiated stage preceding the formation of yin and yang, also known as the "two Principles" (*eryi*). *Qi* written as 炁 indicates the precelestial vital energy; it is used ten times in *Master Incapable*, in the chapters "The Fault of the Sages," "True Cultivation" I, and "Discourse on King Wen," almost always in the context of the formation of the cosmos. The more conventional *qi* 氣 is used nine times, often in the context of the vital energies of the individual human being, but not consistently so. On the different uses of 炁 and 氣, including in *Master Incapable*, see Zhu Yueli 1983.

ii. In the *Daozang*, "shelled" (*jia* 甲) is missing.

iii. Understanding *meng* 濛 ("drizzling mist") as *meng* 蒙 ("simple"). Instead of reading this sentence 濛濛淳淳，其理也居且久矣 as Wang Ming does, I prefer to read it as 濛濛淳淳其理也，居且久矣.

iv. Reading *de* 得 following *Zihui*, instead of *de* 德, as in the *Daozang*.

v. "Established": preferring *jian* 建 (*Daozang*) over *fen* 分 ("to divide," *Zihui*).

vi. Following the *Zihui*, which reads *chan* 鋋 ("short spear") instead of the *Daozang* reading *ding* 鋌 ("barb of an arrow").

vii. Instead of "provoking" (*ji* 激) as in the *Daozang*, the *Zihui* has the inferior reading "unifying" (*yi* 一).

viii. "Oblivious": instead of *wang* 忘, the *Zihui* and later editions copying it read *cang* 藏. The translation would then read "Hide it away" or "Store it up."

ix. Instead of "banished" (*fang* 放) as in the *Daozang*, the *Zihui* reads "attacked" (*fa* 伐). These references to historical or legendary figures make clear that Master Incapable is not only pointing at the crucial role of nonpurposive action in a cosmological or mystical sense, but that he is concerned with how it is put into practice in government. A huge distance seems to separate the hermits, who were unwilling to rule or to serve a ruler, from Yao, Shun, Yu, Qi, Tang and King Wu, some of whom established their own rule after having rebelled against their former master. But in being free of "partial emotions" they did not differ. The theme that nonpurposive action may be translated into seemingly widely different kinds of action will also be pursued in the second and third book, in particular in the chapters "Discourse on King Wen" and "Reply to Huayangzi's Question."

x. The *Daozang* reads "Until the end of their lives, they forget to put to use [the foundation]" (終日忘用). Together with Wang Ming, I opt for the *Zihui* reading (終日妄用).

xi. What is remarkable about this short but important chapter is that non-purposive action is described as if it were the Way. This is reminiscent of a passage in the first *Liezi* chapter (see Graham 1960, 20; Yang 1985, 9–10), which explains the difference between "the begotten and the Begetter of the begotten, shapes and the Shaper of shapes, sounds and the Sounder of sounds." The argument is that that which makes things into what they are—and which *Liezi* describes as nonpurposive action—is itself as endless, as timeless and as intangible as the Way. Ultimately, Master Incapable's inspiration goes back to *Daodejing* 37, which opens with the words: "The Way is constantly without action" (道常無為). Like *Daodejing* 37, this *Master Incapable* chapter also involves the role of desire as the enemy of nonpurposive action and the nameless. The "nameless unworked wood" from *Daodejing* 37 and *Master Incapable*'s "nameless beginning" which will be "shown in the midst of what cannot be seen" both refer to the workings of the Way.

xii. "Moving": instead of *sui* 雖, as in the *Daozang*, the *Zihui* has the clearly inferior *bu* 不.

xiii. "Desire": reading *yu* 欲 (*Zihui*) instead of *gu* 故 (*Daozang*).

xiv. *Xingming*, the life force that can only manifest itself in cooperation with the tangible body, simultaneously has a material and an immaterial dimension. This is suggested by the way in which Master Incapable explains *xing* and *ming*. Inborn nature is equal to *shen* 神, the divine, or the spiritual essence, whereas one's heavenly-ordained lifespan is explained as the *qi*, the vital breath or force. *Shen* is a highly spiritualized form of energy; *qi* has an important material dimension. We shall return to these concepts in the chapter "True Cultivation" III. An excellent article on the meanings of the heavenly-ordained lifespan (*ming*) and its relation with inborn nature (*xing*) in the context of internal alchemy (*neidan* 內丹), but with many references to older Daoist works is Pregadio 2014.

xv. "Abhorred": instead of *wu* 惡 as in the *Daozang*, the *Zihui* reads "dread" (*wei* 畏). "Disturb": reading *gu* 汩 as in the *Zihui*, instead of the inferior *Daozang* reading *dong* 洞. As Zhang Songhui (2005) remarks in his *Master Incapable* edition, the three great Chinese worldviews each proposed their own way of tampering with the temporal limitations of life on earth. Confucianism has a form of posthumous immortality based on one's virtuous deeds and, in some cases, one's literary creations. In Buddhism there is the hope of ending the otherwise infinite series of rebirths which is the result of the production of karma. In Daoism there is the ideal of postmortem immortality or transcendence, the formation of an immortal embryo that can rise up to heaven after the death of the physical body. Against this background, *Zhuangzi* and *Liezi*, in their acceptance of death as part of a larger natural process, may be viewed as exceptions, and the same goes for Master Incapable, who tries to render the fear of dying invalid by claiming that the physical body has always been dead and therefore can no longer die. That Master Incapable adopts this attitude here is perhaps somewhat surprising, for in other chapters (such as "True Cultivation" III) his thinking is in agreement with the equanimity in the face of death expressed in *Zhuangzi*.

xvi. The *Zihui* reading *xu* 煦 ("to spit") is to be preferred over the *Daozang* (*xu* 煦, "warmth of the rising sun").

xvii. Master Incapable's experiment with the cutting into pieces of all people and the subsequent impossibility of reconstituting the original persons may seem somewhat bizarre, but in the end his argument is similar to what is posited in the second *Zhuangzi* chapter, namely that the distinction between "me" and "the others" has no factual basis. In Master Incapable's analysis, because the division of mankind into relatives and nonrelatives is an example of the "forcible application of naming" (we recognize *qiangming*) and, moreover, this division entails an important role for the emotions (another recurring culprit), Master Incapable recommends being oblivious of one another in "what-is-so-of-itself" or naturalness. He does so by referring to the powerful image, occuring twice in *Zhuangzi*, of fish left stranded on the ground as the springs dry up. The fish trying to keep each other alive by spewing moisture at each other are the equivalent of mankind practicing humaneness. It is an act that may seem laudable but that will not change the fact that mankind, once cut off from the source of naturalness, is doomed. See Watson 1968, 87, 163; Guo Qingfan 1985, 272, 522.

xviii. "Free of intentionality" is *wuxin* 無心, or "no-mind," i.e., the absence of thought, emotions, worries, desires, and intentions. As no-mind is an important concept in Chan (Zen) Buddhism, some consider *Master Incapable* to be heavily influenced by Chan. However, this need not be the case. *Daodejing* 49 opens with the words: "The sage has no constant mind of his own" (聖人無常心), *Zhuangzi* 6 enjoins us "not to cast aside the Way through the heart-mind" (不以心捐道), and the first section of *Zhuangzi* 12 quotes an unidentified "Record": "Freed from any intention [*wuxin*] for gain, the spirits and gods will submit" (無心得而鬼神服). *Zhuangzi* 22 contains a dialogue between Nieque 齧缺 and Beiyi 被衣 (Ziporyn translates their names as Gnawgap and Pajama; see Ziporyn 2020, 176; Guo Qingfan 1985, 737–738). Gnawgap asks Pajama about the *dao*, whereupon Pajama starts to explain, but before he is done, Gnawgap falls asleep, and Pajama starts singing merrily. His final words are, in Ziporyn's translation: "Dim and obscure, free of intentions [*wuxin*], unconsultable – what sort of person is this?" (媒媒晦晦，无心而不可與謀。彼何人哉). Moreover, *wuxin* occurs over fifty times in Guo Xiang's highly influential *Zhuangzi* commentary, which Master Incapable seems to have known well, and Guo Xiang can hardly be considered a Chan Buddhist.

xix. I prefer *shi* 式 ("model," "pattern," as in the *Daozang*) to the later *Zihui* emendation *min* 民. Wang Ming is correct in stating that both characters have a similar appearance, but I do believe that *shi* was the original character and not a scribal error for *min*.

xx. What I translate as "Spirit" is *shen* 神, a highly complex notion indicating everything that is divine, godly, or sacred. Mountains, streams, and old trees have their own *shen*, but so do humans, in the form of the body-gods that inhabit us. At the same time it indicates "that quality in humans which may be nurtured and perfected so as to shed one's bodily frame and become a rarified being all of spirit" and "that power or agency which makes possible interaction and relation with nature and with other beings" (see Kroll 2015, 407). For an introduction to *shen*, in relation to *jing* 精 ("essence") and *qi*, see Despeux 2008. The following *Master Incapable* chapter further elucidates "Spirit" by pointing at its relation with vital energy.

xxi. Instead of "supernatural communication" (*lingtong* 靈通), the *Zihui* and other later editions read "communication with the Void" (*xutong* 虛通). Here, Master Incapable returns to one of his favorite themes: the emptiness of the mind, this time using terminology reminiscent of *Mencius*. "Flood-like" (*haoran* 浩然) recalls Mencius' statement: "I am skillful in nourishing my flood-like vital breath" (我善養吾浩然之氣) in the first part of Book II of *Mencius* (see Legge 1895, 189). For the second time, Master Incapable also refers to the "utmost harmony" (*zhihe* 至和); the first time was in "Being Free of Worries." In the first *Liezi* chapter, this notion is connected with infancy: "In infancy his energies are concentrated and his inclinations at one—the ultimate of harmony. Other things do not harm him, nothing in him can add to the virtue in him" (其在嬰孩，氣專志一，和之至也：物不傷焉，德莫加焉.) See Graham 1960, 23; Yang 1985, 21. The source is *Daodejing* 55, where the infant's ability to cry all day long without getting hoarse is described as the "utmost in harmony."

Text-critical Endnotes to Book II

xxii. The *Zihui* and other later editions omit the characters *yi cheng* 已成 ("have been built").

xxiii. "Why": understanding 何謂 as 何為.

xxiv. Instead of *dai* 逮 ("coming to," hence "being a match for," as in the *Daozang*), the *Zihui* reads *jin* 進 ("advance").

xxv. Instead of *ling* 零 ("fall gently") as in the *Daozang*, the *Zihui* reads *yun* 隕 ("descend," "decline").

xxvi. *Shuai* 率, as in the *Daozang*, is generally considered to be an error and replaced by *zu* 卒 ("finally"). I prefer the *Daozang* reading, though.

xxvii. The repeated "fraudulence" or "fraudulent" is *wang* 妄, which may also denote "frivolous," "groundless," or "preposterous."

xxviii. Instead of *bao* 暴 ("violence," as in the *Daozang*), the *Zihui* reads *si* 肆 ("wanton behavior").

xxix. Preferring *chang* 嘗 ("to attempt") as in the *Daozang* over the homophone 常 ("constant") as in the *Zihui*.

xxx. Instead of *pu* 暴 ("exposes") as in the *Daozang*, the *Zihui* reads *shu* 舒 ("to spread out"). Both readings are possible.

xxxi. Master Incapable found his inspiration in *Records of the Historian*, which devotes chapter 61 to the reclusive brothers (see Nienhauser 1994–2019, vol. VII, 1–8). Whether Bo Yi and Shu Qi may be considered wise hermits has long been a topic of debate. In this context, see Vervoorn 1983. In the *Analects*, Confucius indirectly approved of the actions of King Wu, but from another point of view he also had a certain measure of admiration for Bo Yi and Shu Qi. Master Incapable's attitude is quite the opposite, as he condemns both King Wu (for being driven by a desire for power) and the reclusive brothers (for being driven by a desire for a good reputation). Master Incapable's slightly weird rhetorical maneuver of seeming to address Bo Yi and Shu Qi directly has been interpreted by some (see, e.g., Zhang Songhui 2005, 62) as a means to indirectly criticize the author's End-Tang contemporaries. It is worthwhile to compare Master Incapable's criticism of the reclusive brothers with that of Ruan Ji, in his "Poetic Exposition on Mount Shouyang" (*Shouyangshan fu* 首陽山賦). "Why were they praised for fellow-feeling and right?" wonders Ruan Ji. He continues: "They acted rashly regarding lifespans and were not at ease, contesting for good name as their measure." See Owen and Swartz 2017, 170–175, esp. 173.

xxxii. The word order in the *Daozang* (是謂) is to be preferred over that in the *Zihui* (謂是).

xxxiii. The characters for "depending on allotment" (懸乎分) as in the *Daozang* are missing in the *Zihui* and other later editions.

xxxiv. "The wisdom of": the reading *zhi* 之 in the *Daozang* is to be preferred over the *shang* 上 as in the *Zihui*.

xxxv. Instead of "Lu and Wey" (魯衛) as in the *Daozang*, the *Zihui* reads "in Wey" (於衛). Zigong was prime minister in both Lu and Wey, but served in Wey only after Confucius's death.

xxxvi. "Graciously": reading the erroneous *de* 得 (*Daozang*) as the homophonous 德 (as in the *Zihui* and all later editions).

xxxvii. Fan Li draws attention to a principle we know as "autonomous transformation" (*duhua* 獨化). This means that all things are what they are as the result of a natural, inherent tendency to be so, and that things are unable to create or cause other things. This principle had already been formulated by the early *Daodejing* commentator Zhuang Zun 莊遵 (c. 83 BC–c. 10 CE) and by the philosopher Wang Chong (27–c. 97), but it is Guo Xiang who is now chiefly remembered as its propagator. In his commentary to *Zhuangzi* 2,

Guo Xiang writes: "Since nothingness is nothing, it cannot produce being. Before being itself is produced, it cannot produce other beings. Then by whom are things produced? They spontaneously produce themselves, that is all. This does not mean that there is an 'I' that produces them. The 'I' cannot produce things, and things cannot produce the 'I.' The 'I' exists of itself, and because it is self-existent, we call it natural. Everything is what it is by nature, not through taking any action." And in his commentary to *Zhuangzi* 22, he states: "What came into existence before there were things? If I say yin and yang came first, then, since yin and yang are themselves things, what came before them? Suppose I say the natural [*ziran*] came first? But the natural is only things being themselves. Suppose I say perfect Dao came first? But perfect Dao is perfect nothingness. Since it is nothingness, how can it come before anything else? Then what came before it? There must be another thing, and so on, endlessly. We must understand that things are what they are spontaneously and are not caused by something else." (Both fragments adapted from the translation by Wing-Tsit Chan, in De Bary and Bloom 1999, 386–387).

In keeping with this line of thought, Master Incapable posits that though spring brings warmth, coming to life is done by all things spontaneously, and though winter brings cold, it is things themselves that spontaneously die. Master Incapable's reasoning in this chapter, together with his view in the first chapter of Book I that all creatures are the result of the spontaneous interaction of yin and yang, earned him a place in Wang Yousan's 王友三 *An Historical Outline of Chinese Atheism* (1982, 191–192).

xxxviii. "Disciple": *qi tu* 其徒 (*Daozang*) is to be preferred over *qi fei* 其非 (*Zihui*). Song Yu 宋玉 (third century BC), to whom a number of poems in the *Verses of Chu* are attributed, is often mentioned as Qu Yuan's disciple. He is not normally considered a hermit. In most accounts, such as Qu Yuan's biography in chapter 84 of *Records of the Historian* and in *Lives of Eminent Gentlemen*, an anonymous fisherman unsuccessfully tries to talk Qu Yuan out of suicide. See Nienhauser 1994–2019, vol. VII, 295–302.

xxxix. "Zealous": preferring *wu* 務 as in the *Daozang* over *li* 立 ("to establish") as in *Zihui* and other later editions.

xl. "Favors": preferring *hui* 惠 as in the *Daozang* over *zhi* 直 ("straight") as in the *Zihui*.

xli. "Order": the *Daozang* has *liluan* 理亂; the *Zihui* omits the *luan*.

xlii. "Preserved": preferring *cun* 存 in the *Zihui* edition over *xiao* 孝, probably a clerical error in the *Daozang*.

xliii. "Dismiss": the *Daozang* version (*chu* 黜) is to be preferred over the *dian* 點 ("to dot") in the *Zihui*.

xliv. The *Zihui* reads: "*Not* obtaining one's allotment and feeling sad because of it" (不得其所分又悲之者).

xlv. "Can": the *Daozang* does not have the *neng* 能 found in all later editions.

xlvi. Both the *Daozang* and the *Zihui* read 乃復商山. According to Wang Ming 1981, 27, the *Baizi quanshu* 白子全書 and the *Zishu baijia* 子書百家 editions read 乃復隱商山.

xlvii. Zhang Liang obtained immortal status, and is traditionally considered the eighth-generation ancestor of Zhang Daoling. The meeting between Emperor Gaozu and the four hermits is recounted in *Records of the Historian* 55.2047 (see Watson 1993, 109–110). The four hoaryheads are among the most controversial recluses in all of Chinese history. Critics found it hard to believe that the four old wise men, who had once shown their uncompromising resolve when they absconded to the Shangluo mountains during the brutal Qin regime, allowed themselves to be implicated in what was little more than a palace intrigue. Tellingly, the episode is not mentioned in *Lives of Eminent Gentlemen*, which focuses entirely on the old men's reclusion under the Qin and the unsuccessful attempt by the first Han emperor to invite them to court. The Neo-Confucian philosopher Wang Yangming 王陽明 (1472–1528) even went so far as to suggest that the four greybeards whom Zhang Liang attracted to court were actually con artists impersonating the genuine recluses. See Vervoorn 1990, 96–100 and Berkowitz 2000, 64–80. Rapp (1979, 96) perceives the attitude of the four hoaryheads as essentially cynical: in agreeing "to serve the evil Queen Mother and her henchman the Marquis of Liu," the foursome do the "dirty work" for the Empress, "to the point where her son ascended the throne and her enemies were eliminated." Rapp further speculates that it is perhaps because of this cynical attitude that Hsiao Kung-chuan made the claim that Chinese Daoist anarchism was nothing but a doctrine of despair. Zarrow (1990, 10) and Hoston (1994, 159) hold similar views on Master Incapable's perceived cynicism or nihilism.

xlviii. The *zi* 子 ("you") in the *Daozang* is replaced with *ke* 可 ("can") in the *Zihui*.

xlix. The *Daozang* reading *tie* 帖 ("peaceable") is replaced by the homophonous reading 帖 ("settle," "stable") in the *Zihui* and other later editions.

l. "An escort in front": instead of *qu* 驅 ("spur on,") as in the *Daozang*, the *Zihui* reads *cu* 簇 ("bring to a stop"). "chilis and orchids": in the *Zihui* edition, *jiaolan* 椒蘭 as in the *Daozang* is replaced with *gaoxian* 膏鮮 ("fatty and fresh").

li. "Embarrassed": following the *Daozang*, which reads *can* 憗, while the *Zihui* and other later editions read *wu* 悟, "awoke." The tone of this story is grim. Yan Guang initially smiles, but he keeps repeating that the emperor is merely trying to entice him with things that may appeal to the conventionally minded, but not to one who is "submerged in the Great Void and feeds on the Great Harmony." As in the first part of "Offering Proof of Absurdities," wealth, power and status—in other words, things which in Master Incapable's vision are the result of "enforced naming"—are being attacked with an insistence typical only for the *Zhuangzi*'s primitivist chapters. Master Incapable is as critical of Guangwu (the "successful" new emperor) as he is of Wang Mang (the usurper) and the Gengshi Emperor (the "failed" new emperor)—all of them "seeking to be revered by the central states, and feeling no concern whatsoever over all-under-heaven." I agree with Zhang Songhui (2005, 8) in reading this as evidence that neither the Tang court nor the rebel Huang Chao could count on Master Incapable's sympathy.

lii. "Comprehend": the *zhi* 知 (*Daozang*) is replaced by *ru* 如 ("being like") in the *Zihui*. "Cannot equal": interpreting *qi* 期 as *xiangyue* 相約 or *xiangbi* 相比, as does Zhang Songhui (2005, 110).

liii. The wording here is rather unclear. Following the *Daozang* reading *shi bu lei* 仕不累 instead of the *shi ze lei* 仕則累 of later emendations (following the *Zihui*), one would have to interpret this sentence as "Serving in office need not be troublesome, whereas not serving might mean exactly that."

liv. Both the *Daozang* and the *Zihui* read *xing* 醒 ("to sober up"); only the *Zishu baijia* has *cheng* 酲 ("hangover, from drink").

Text-critical Endnotes to Book III

lv. In the thirteenth-century *Comprehensive Mirror of Perfected Immortals and of Those Who Embodied the Way Through the Ages* (*Lishi zhenxian tidao tongjian* 歷世真仙體道通鑑), Sun Deng and Xi Kang have extensive biographical accounts side by side in chapter 34. See Campany 2009, 244. Xi Kang himself was convinced that, through a combination of ascetic practices, man would be able to live to an age of at least two hundred years. See his debate with the *Zhuangzi* commentator Xiang Xiu 向秀 (c. 221–300), translated in Henricks 1983, 21–70.

lvi. "Immersed in": the *xi* 兮 (a rhythmic particle) in the *Daozang* is obviously a mistake and has been corrected to *hu* 乎 in the *Zihui*.

lvii. Instead of *nao* 撓 as in the *Daozang*, the *Zihui* reads *pi* 疲 ("exhausted").

lviii. Naundorf (1972, 122) and Rapp (2012, 254) assume that the falling here is done by the rain. But the verb used is *duo* 墮 (and not *xia* 下), as in the passage in the fourth part of the chapter "True Cultivation," where it is stated that if birds were to set their minds on flying, they would certainly fall.

lix. It is not hard to read this chapter as a form of consolation for all those who fail the highest imperial examinations and realize they will never become government officials. Fish who become dragons may be able to attract rain, but they exhaust their power, whereas the ordinary fish, who are unable to climb the Dragon Gate, lead a life free of stress and danger. The two categories have their own allotment, and that should be suitable to all. Note also how Master Incapable provides a materialist or naturalistic explanation for the formation of clouds and rain. At the same time, he once more illustrates the principle of being "without intentionality," as the mechanism at work here is one of spontaneous influence and does not involve creatures setting their mind to something. Master Incapable possibly echoes a fragment of Guo Xiang's commentary to *Zhuangzi* 2 (see Guo Qingfan 1985, 88, n. 27). Guo Xiang advises against striving for what is "outside" oneself; one should rather "stop at one's own inborn nature" (止乎本性). Striving for what is outside oneself, according to Guo Xiang, "can be likened to something round imitating something square, or to fish emulating birds" (譬猶以圓學方，以魚慕鳥). The closer one tries to get to what one is not, the further one becomes separated from substantiality.

lx. "Hostile": the *Zihui* reading *ji* 疾 and the homophonous 嫉 in the *Daozang* are both possible.

lxi. Later editions, such as the *Zihui*, emended the original *hou qi shen* 後其身 (*Daozang*) to *quan qi shen* 全其身 ("keep myself intact"), which does not make sense, as *hou qi shen* is a clear reference to *Daodejing* 7: "The sage puts his own person last, and yet his person is found in front."

lxii. "Once": reading *chang* 嘗 as in the *Zihui* instead of the probable copying error *dang* 當 as in the *Daozang*.

lxiii. "Hemp": the *Daozang* reads *cui* 縗 ("unhemmed hemp bib, worn in mourning"), the *Zihui* reads *shuai* 衰.

lxiv. I find the interpretations by Naundorf (1972, 125), Rapp (2012, 256), and Zhang Songhui (2005, 145) of the latter part of this sentence unsatisfactory. I take 又將誰付耶 to be a rhetorical question meaning literally, "Whom would you turn yourself over to any longer?" Hence my translation "without becoming dependent on anything at all."

lxv. "Indolent": reading *sui* 隨 as *duo* 惰.

lxvi. One may object that the reasoning behind Master Incapable's plea for "no-mind" is a bit weak. It is not because the mind is invisible that it is unable to exert its influence.

lxvii. The *ji* 紀 in the title (紀見) is synonymous with 記, "to record" or "write down."

lxviii. "Highest power": *shangde* 上德. What does Master Incapable have in mind here? *Shangde* is mentioned twice in the *Daodejing*, the first time in the enigmatic verse 38, where it is often interpreted as meaning that the man of highest power does not manifest his power and therefore has power, whereas the man of lowest power clings to power, not wanting to lose it, and therefore lacks power. In *Daodejing* 38 the highest power is also associated with *wuwei*, but its message is hard to interpret because of the existence of different versions. A silk manuscript from Mawangdui reads: "The highest power is free of purposive action and does not have ulterior motives" (or: and therefore nothing needs to be done) 上德無為而無以為也.

In the Heshanggong version, this is expanded to: "The highest power is free of purposive action and does not have ulterior motives; the lowest power takes action and does have ulterior motives" (or: and therefore some things need to be done) 上德無為而無以為，下德為之而有以為. In the so-called "old text" version preserved by the mathematician, astrologer and Daoist priest Fu Yi 傅奕 (555–639), another variation is found: "The highest power is free of purposive action, and therefore nothing is left undone; the lowest power takes action, and therefore some things need to be done" 上德無為而無不為，下德為之而有以為. In any case, we may safely understand "the highest power" as indicating *wuwei*, which in *Master Incapable* occupies a place so central that it is described as if it were the Way itself (see the chapter "Illuminating the Foundation"). Further, in *Daodejing* 41, the highest power is likened to a valley, an image of emptiness, and thus of virtuality or potentiality, or, in the words of Heshanggong: "The man of highest power is like a deep valley; he is not ashamed of being defiled." And of course one must also think here of the description of the time of "perfect power" in the primitivist ninth chapter of the *Zhuangzi*, when means of communication did not yet exist, and humans lived side by side with the other animals, free of desire and able to realize their true nature.

lxix. Preferring 人家將凶則梟來鳴 as in the *Zihui* version to the problematic 人將家凶則來鳴 as in the *Daozang*.

lxx. Instead of *lu* 錄 ("make note of") as in the *Daozang*, the *Zihui* reads *zui* 罪 ("blame").

lxxi. The *mao* 貌 ("appearance") in the *Daozang* is to be preferred over the *qie* 且 ("moreover") in the *Zihui* and other later editions.

lxxii. Preferring the *Daozang* reading (*jie* 節, "moderate," hence "well-regulated") over the *Zihui* reading *shan* 善 ("be good at").

lxxiii. One is tempted here to read the *Daozang*'s *gu* 固 ("definitely") as the *yin* 因 ("being founded or based on") of most later versions. The meaning of the sentence is clear, though: civilized things are a watered-down, diluted version of the original "strong drink" (*zhou* 酎).

lxxiv. Wang Ming (1981, 14) has described *Master Incapable* as a "diary of a madman" (*kuangren riji* 狂人日記), referring to Lu Xun's 魯迅 (1881–1936) famous short story of 1918, which was itself inspired by Nikolai Gogol's (1809–1852) story of the same title. With his chapter about a lone madman (who is of course Master Incapable himself) who perceives reality more clearly than all who surround him, Master Incapable predates Lu Xun by more than a millennium. But he was not the first one in Chinese history to write on this theme. It is highly probable that Master Incapable was himself influenced by the penultimate, anti-Confucian anecdote in the third *Liezi* chapter about the son of Mr. Pang of Qin, who took white to be black, sweet to be bitter, and wrong to be right (see Graham 1960, 72–73; Yang 1985, 111–112). Persuaded to travel to Lu so that the Confucians there could try and cure his son, Mr. Pang, while passing through Chen 陳, meets with Laozi and tells him about his son's affliction. Laozi convinces Mr. Pang to go back home and refrain from wasting his money, because in a world where everyone is "deluded about right and wrong, and confused about benefit and harm," delusion has become the norm, and all the "sick" people consider the remaining healthy ones as sick. It is easy to discard the madman's attitude as an egoism-based unwillingness to communicate, but that would be a grave misunderstanding of the essence of Master Incapable's message. The madman's extreme "semantic relativism"—all naming is arbitrary, so feel free to invent your own language—is first and foremost an expression of a strong desire for naturalness, fewer constraints and, in the final analysis, less violence. In his important *Balanced Discourses* essay, "Naturalness," Wang Chong mentions that in the days of the earliest rulers of high antiquity, people referred to themselves now as horses, then as cows. Wang considered this kind of naming to be a sign of a life permeated by the satisfaction accompanying great simplicity (see Forke 1907, 100; Beijing daxue lishixi 1979, 1042–1043). Master Incapable would have agreed with that position, as he would have agreed with Zhuangzi's views on language being a pernicious means of dividing or separating, thereby rendering invisible the fundamental unity of everything. On the latter topic, see Levi 2010.

lxxv. Preferring the *Daozang* reading *er* 鮞 ("fish roe") over a variant character with the 虫 ("insect") radical in the *Zihui*.

lxxvi. The inspiration for this piece on the benefits of nonpurposive action comes from chapter 17 of the legalist classic *Han Feizi*. The final sentence is not easy to interpret, because of the presence of the character *jian* 間 ("space between"). Zhang Songhui's (2005, 163) interpretation is that only by cherishing all people on earth in a disinterested manner can the profit-seeking of the coffin maker and the doctor be avoided, and thus one's aim resides entirely in helping the dead and curing the sick. Rapp's (2012, 259) interpretation is similar. Naundorf evades the problem by not translating a part of the original phrase. The question is: why did Wunengzi not simply use the words *zaiyu* 在於 ("reside in"), instead of *zai . . . zhijian* 在 . . . 之間 ("reside somewhere in between . . .")? A possible answer may be found in the first anecdote of *Zhuangzi* 20, where a tree gets to live out its natural years because it is worthless, whereas a goose that cannot cackle is killed for exactly the same reason. Asked by his disciples what position would be his, Zhuangzi replies: "I'd probably take a position halfway between worth and worthlessness" 材與不材之間 (see Watson 1968, 209). Zhuangzi then goes on to explain that a position halfway between worth and worthlessness is not safe either, and his final advice is to stay within the realm of the Way and its Power.

lxxvii. The *Zihui* and other later versions omit the *jian* 繭 ("cocoon") found in the *Daozang* version.

lxxviii. Master Incapable combines *Zhuangzi*'s cult of uselessness with an argument made in the final *Liezi* chapter (see Graham 1960, 178–179; Yang 1985, 269–270). Before going on a journey, a man offers a banquet to his guests and, looking at the food, says, in Graham's words: "How generous heaven is to mankind! It grows the five grains and breeds the fish and birds for the use of man." All those present agree, except for a twelve-year old boy, who objects: "It is not as your lordship says. The myriad things between heaven and earth, born in the same way that we are, do not differ from us in kind. One kind is no nobler than another; it is simply that the stronger and cleverer rule the weaker and sillier. Things take it in turns to eat each other, but they are not bred for each other's sake . . ." This takes us back to *Master Incapable*'s first chapter (see p. 9). Somewhat surprisingly, no *Liezi* commentator seems to have noticed that the words of the twelve-year old boy, who happens to belong to the Bao 鮑 clan, are similar to the opening argument of proto-anarchist Bao Jingyan in chapter 48 of *The Master Who Embraces Simplicity, Outer Chapters*. The young Bao who says that the stronger and cleverer rule the weaker and sillier may be the same person as the "student Bao" (he is after all called "Bao sheng" 鮑生 in *The Master Who Embraces Simplicity*) who remarks that the strong oppressed the weak and the cunning tricked the innocent. Both Baos also agree on animals not being put on earth in order to be enjoyed by humans. And once again, the influence of the "Naturalness" chapter from *Balanced Discourses* may be seen here (see Forke 1907, 92; Beijing daxue lishixi 1979, 1027). Wang Chong also treats the question of nature's utility for mankind, rejecting the opinion that "Heaven produces grain for the purpose of feeding mankind, and silk and hemp to clothe them," as that would not be in accordance with the principle of naturalness or spontaneity.

Bibliography

Principal editions

Wunengzi 无能子. *Zhengtong Daozang* 正統道藏 [Daoist Canon of the Zhengtong Reign Period], reprinted 1926.

Wunengzi 无能子. *Zihui* 子彙 [The Masters Collocated]. *Yuan Ming shanben congshu.*

Wunengzi 無能子. *Zhuzi huihan* 諸子彙函 [Casket Collecting Various Masters].

Wang Ming 王明, ed. 1981. *Wunengzi jiaozhu* 无能子校注 [*Master Incapable* with Textual Criticism and Annotation]. Zhonghua shuju.

Zhang Songhui 張松輝. 2005. *Xinyi* Wunengzi 新譯无能子 [*Master Incapable* with a New Translation]. Sanmin shuju.

Translations

De Meyer, Jan. 2011. *Nietskunner. Het taoïsme en de bevrijding van de geest* [Wunengzi. Daoism and the Liberation of the Mind]. Augustus.

Naundorf, Gert. 1972. "Aspekte des anarchischen Gedankens in China. Darstellung der Lehre und Übersetzung des Textes Wu Neng Tzu" [Aspects of Anarchist Thought in China. A Presentation of the Teachings and Translation of the text *Wunengzi*]. Unpublished doctoral thesis, Julius-Maximilians-Universität Würzburg.

Rapp, John A. 2012. *Daoism and Anarchism. Critiques of State Autonomy in Ancient and Modern China*, translated by Catrina Siu. Continuum.

Woolley, Nathan. 1997. "*Wunengzi* and the Early *Zhuangzi* Commentaries." Unpublished bachelors honors thesis, Faculty of Asian Studies, Australian National University.

Secondary Scholarship

Bu Jinzhi 步近智. 1980. "Tang mo Wudai Pi Rixiu, Wunengzi, Tan Qiao de jinbu si-xiang" 唐末五代皮日休，无能子，譚峭的進步思想 [The Progressive Thought of Pi Rixiu, Wunengzi, and Tan Qiao in the End Tang and Five Dynasties]. *Lishi jiaoxue* 歷史教學 12: 7–10.

De Meyer, Jan. 2004. "*Wuneng zi.*" In *The Taoist Canon: A Historical Companion to the Daozang*, edited by Kristofer Schipper and Franciscus Verellen, 317–318.

Hsiao, Kung-chuan (Xiao Gongquan). 1936. "Anarchism in Chinese Political Thought." *T'ien Hsia Monthly* III (3): 249–263.

Jiang An 江安. 1983. "*Wunengzi* pianmu xiaokao" 无能子篇目小考 [A Short Examination of *Master Incapable*'s Chapter Titles]. *Shehui kexue zhanxian* 社會科學戰線 2: 345.

Jiang Yiwei 姜亦煒. 2018. "Junchen pipan, wutuobang yu wuwei zhengzhi—Jiyu Tang mo *Wunengzi* de wenben fenxi" 君臣批判，烏托邦與無為政治—基於唐末《无能子》的文本分析 [Criticism of Rulers and Subjects, Utopia and Government by Non-Interference: An Analysis Based upon the End Tang Text *Master Incapable*]. *Zhonggong Hangzhou shiwei dangxiao xuebao* 中共杭州市委黨校學報 4: 68–74.

Li Guangfu 李光福. 2005. "Lun Wunengzi zhexue de shengtai lunli yiyun" 論无能子哲學的生態倫理意蘊 [A Discussion of the Implied Ecological Ethics in *Master Incapable*'s Philosophy]. *Dongnan daxue xuebao* 東南大學學報 7 (1): 23–26.

Li Junheng 李俊恒. 1987. "*Wunengzi* jiqi zai Tang mo sixiangshi shang de diwei" 《无能子》及其在唐末思想史上的地位 [*Master Incapable* and its Position in the History of End Tang Thought]. *Xuchang shizhuan xuebao* 許昌師專學報 1: 38–45.

Li Xi 李曦. 1985. "*Wunengzi*" 无能子 [Master Incapable]. In *Zhongguo gudai yiming zhexue mingzhu pingshu* 中國古代佚名哲學名著評述 [A Critical Narration of Famous Philosophical Works of Ancient China by Unknown Authors], edited by Xin Guanjie 辛冠洁 and Ding Jiansheng 丁健生, 391–426. Qi-Lu shushe.

Naundorf, Gert. 1968. "Zum anarchischen Gedanken in China" [On Anarchist Thought in China]. *Papers of the XIX International Congress of Chinese Studies*, 57–62. Ostasien-Institut der Ruhr-Universität Bochum.

Penny, Benjamin. 2008. "Wuneng zi." *The Routledge Encyclopedia of Taoism*, edited by Fabrizio Pregadio, 1059–1060. Routledge.

Quan Genxian 全根先. 1991. "*Wunengzi* de sixiang jiqi ziliao laiyuan" 《无能子》的思想及其資料來源 [*Master Incapable*'s Thought and Its Source Materials]. *Zhongguo daojiao* 中國道教 1: 38–43.

Sun Gongjin 孫功進. 2010. "Zhuangzi sixiang dui Wunengzi de yingxiang" 《莊子》思想對《无能子》的影響 [The Influence of *Zhuangzi*'s Thought on *Master Incapable*]. *Henan keji daxue xuebao* 河南科技大學學報 28 (6): 27–31.

Tan Min 譚敏. 2011. "Tang mo Wudai de yinyi xianxiang yu daojiaotu de huiying" 唐末五代的隱逸現象與道教徒的回應 [The Phenomenon of Reclusion in the End Tang and Five Dynasties and the Response of Daoists]. *Beijing huagong daxue xuebao* 北京化工大學學報 (*Shehui kexue ban* 社會科學版) 3: 47–51.

Zhao Jun 趙俊. 1999. "Wan Tang sixiangjie sanjie" 晚唐思想界三傑 [Three Heroes of the Late Tang World of Thought]. *Zhongguo shehui kexueyuan yan-jiushengyuan xuebao* 中國社會科學院研究生院學報 6: 67–74.

Zhu Yueli 朱越利. 1983. "Shilun *Wunengzi*" 試論无能子 [A Tentative Discussion of *Master Incapable*]. *Shijie zongjiao yanjiu* 世界宗教研究 1: 107–122.

Works Cited

Allan, Sarah. 1972–1973. "The Identities of Taigong Wang 太公望 in Zhou and Han Literature." *Monumenta Serica* 30: 57–99.

Ames, Roger T. 1983. "Is Political Taoism Anarchism?" *Journal of Chinese Philosophy* 10: 27–47.

Assandri, Friederike. 2009. *Beyond the Daode Jing: Twofold Mystery in Tang Daoism.* Three Pines Press.

Balazs, Etienne. 1964. "Nihilistic Revolt or Mystical Escapism: Currents of Thought in China During the Third Century A.D." In idem, *Chinese Civilization and Bureaucracy*, translated by H. M. Wright and edited by Arthur F. Wright, 226–254. Yale University Press.

Barrett, T. H. 1996. *Taoism Under the T'ang. Religion & Empire During the Golden Age of Chinese History.* Wellsweep.

Bauer, Wolfgang. 1974. *China und die Hoffnung auf Glück. Paradiese, Utopien, Idealvorstellungen in der Geistesgeschichte Chinas* [China and the Search for Happiness. Recurring Themes in Four Thousand Years of Chinese Cultural History]. Deutscher Taschenbuch Verlag.

Beijing daxue lishixi *Lunheng* zhushi xiaozu 北京大學歷史系論衡注釋小組, ed. 1979. *Lunheng zhushi* 論衡注釋 [Balanced Discourses, with Explanatory Notes]. Zhonghua shuju.

Benn, Charles. 1991. *The Cavern-Mystery Transmission: A Taoist Ordination Rite of A.D. 711.* University of Hawai'i Press.

Benn, Charles. 2002. *China's Golden Age: Everyday Life in the Tang Dynasty.* Oxford University Press.

Berkowitz, Alan J. 2000. *Patterns of Disengagement: The Practice and Portrayal of Reclusion in Early Medieval China.* Stanford University Press.

Birch, Cyril, ed. 1965. *Anthology of Chinese Literature.* Grove Press.

Boutonnet, Olivier. 2021. *Le Char de nuages: Erémitisme et randonnées célestes chez Wu Yun, taoïste du VIIIᵉ siècle* [The Chariot of Clouds: Eremitism and Celestial Rambling in the Works of Wu Yun, Eighth-Century Daoist]. Les Belles Lettres.

Bujard, Marianne. 2000. "Le culte de Wangzi Qiao ou la longue carrière d'un immortel [The Cult of Wangzi Qiao or the Long Career of an Immortal]." *Etudes chinoises* 19: 115–158.

Campany, Robert Ford. 2009. *Making Transcendents: Ascetics and Social Memory in Early Medieval China.* University of Hawai'i Press.

Chen Yumou 陳禹謀. *Pian zhi* 駢志 [A Treatise in Pairs]. *Siku quanshu* 四庫全書 ed.

Ch'en, Kenneth K. S. 1956. "The Economic Background of the Hui-ch'ang Suppression of Buddhism." *Harvard Journal of Asiatic Studies* 19: 67–105.

Dalby, Michael T. 1979. "Court politics in late T'ang times." In *The Cambridge History of China*. Vol. 3, edited by Denis Twitchett, 561–681. Cambridge University Press.

De Bary, Wm. Theodore and Irene Bloom, comps. 1999. *Sources of Chinese Tradition* Vol. 1. Columbia University Press.

De Meyer, Jan. 1992–1993. "Confucianism and Daoism in the Political Thought of Luo Yin." *T'ang Studies* 10–11: 67–80.

De Meyer, Jan. 1996. "'Using the Past to Disparage the Present': Luo Yin and his *Slanderous Writings.*" *Chinese Culture* 37 (1): 69–85.

De Meyer Jan. 2006. *Wu Yun's Way: Life and Works of an Eighth-Century Daoist Master.* Brill.

Denecke, Wiebke. 2010. *The Dynamics of Masters Literature: Early Chinese Thought from Confucius to Han Feizi.* Harvard University Asia Center.

Denecke, Wiebke. 2017. "Masters (*zi* 子)." In *The Oxford Handbook of Classical Chinese Literature (1000 BCE–900 CE)*, edited by Wiebke Denecke, Wai-Yee Li, and Xiaofei Tian, 201–218. Oxford University Press.

Despeux, Catherine. 2008. "*Jing, qi, shen.*" In *The Routledge Encyclopedia of Taoism*, edited by Fabrizio Pregadio, 562–565. Routledge.

Dirlik, Arif. 1991. *Anarchism in the Chinese Revolution.* University of California Press.

Durrant, Stephen, Wai-yee Lee and David Schaberg, trans. 2006. *Zuo Tradition/ Zuozhuan: Commentary on the "Spring and Autumn Annals."* University of Washington Press.

Fang Jiliu 方積六. 1983. *Huang Chao qiyi kao* 黃巢起義考 [*A Study of the Huang Chao Uprising*]. Zhongguo shehui kexue chubanshe.

Forke, Alfred. 1907. *Lun-hêng. Part I. Philosophical Essays of Wang Ch'ung.* Harrassowitz, Luzac & Co., Kelly & Walsh.

Forke, Alfred. 1911. *Lun-hêng. Part II. Miscellaneous Essays of Wang Ch'ung.* Harrassowitz, Luzac & Co., Kelly & Walsh.

Forke, Alfred. 1925. *The World-Conception of the Chinese.* Probsthain.

Forke, Alfred. 1964. *Geschichte der mittelalterlichen chinesischen Philosophie* [History of Medieval Chinese Philosophy]. Friederichsen, De Gruyter.

Franke, Otto. 1961. *Geschichte des Chinesischen Reiches*, Bd. II, 2. Aufl. [History of the Chinese Empire, Vol. II, second edition]. De Gruyter.

Fu, Lo-shu. 1965. "Teng Mu: A Forgotten Chinese Philosopher." *T'oung Pao* 52: 35–96.

Graham, A. C. 1989. *Disputers of the Tao: Philosophical Argument in Ancient China.* Open Court.

Graham, A. C., trans. 1960. *The Book of Lieh-tzu.* John Murray.

Guo Qingfan 郭慶藩, ed. 1985. *Zhuangzi jishi* 莊子集釋 [*Zhuangzi* with Collected Commentaries]. Zhonghua shuju.

Hendrischke, Barbara. 2000. "Early Daoist Movements." In *Daoism Handbook*, edited by Livia Kohn, 134–164. Brill.

Henricks, Robert G. 1983. *Philosophy and Argumentation in Third-Century China: The Essays of Hsi K'ang.* Princeton University Press.

Holzman, Donald. 1976. *Poetry and Politics: The Life and Works of Juan Chi (A.D. 210–263).* Cambridge University Press.

Hoston, Germaine. 1994. *The State, Identity, and the National Question in China and Japan.* Princeton University Press.

Hou Han shu 後漢書 [History of the Later Han]. 1973. Fan Ye 范曄, comp., 398–446. Zhonghua shuju.

Hu Rulei 胡如雷. 1979. *Tangmo nongmin zhanzheng* 唐末農民戰爭 [*The Peasant Wars of the End of the Tang*]. Zhonghua shuju.

Huangfu Mi 皇甫謐. *Gaoshi zhuan* 高士傳 [Lives of Eminent Gentlemen]. *Sibu beiyao* 四部備要 ed.

Ji Yun 紀昀 et al., rpt. 1986. *Siku quanshu* 四庫全書 [*Complete Library of the Four Repositories*]. Rpt. Taiwan Shangwu yinshuguan.

Kirkland, Russell. 2008. "Sima Chengzhen." In *The Routledge Encyclopedia of Taoism*, edited by Fabrizio Pregadio, 911-914. Routledge.

Kohn, Livia. 2010. *Sitting in Oblivion: The Heart of Daoist Meditation*. Three Pines Press.

Kohn, Livia and Russell Kirkland. 2000. "Daoism in the Tang (618–907)." In *Daoism Handbook*, edited by Livia Kohn, 339–383. Brill.

Kroll, Paul W. 2015. *A Student's Dictionary of Classical and Medieval Chinese*. Brill.

Legge, James, 1895, rpt. 1970. *The Works of Mencius*. Dover.

Levi, Jean. 2004. *Eloge de l'anarchie par deux excentriques chinois* [Praise of Anarchy by Two Chinese Excentrics]. Editions de l'Encyclopédie des Nuisances.

Levi, Jean. 2010. "Zhuangzi et l'enfer du politique" [Zhuangzi and the Hell of Politics]. *Etudes chinoises* 29 : 39–68.

Li Dingguang 李定廣. 2006. *Tang mo Wudai luanshi wenxue yanjiu* 唐末五代亂世文學研究 [Studies in the Literature of the Turbulent Times of the End-Tang and the Five Dynasties]. Zhongguo shehui kexue chubanshe.

Littlejohn, Ronnie. 2011. "The *Liezi*'s Use of the Lost *Zhuangzi*." In *Riding the Wind with Liezi: New Perspectives on the Daoist Classic*, edited by Ronnie Littlejohn and Jeffrey Dippmann, 31–49. State University of New York Press.

Liu Wu-chi and Irving Yucheng Lo, eds. 1975. *Sunflower Splendor: Three Thousand Years of Chinese Poetry*. Indiana University Press.

Lu Longqi 陸隴其. *Sishu jiangyi kunmian lu* 四書講義困勉錄 [Constraints and Efforts in Elucidating the Meaning of the Four Books]. *Siku quanshu* ed.

Lü Wuzhi 呂武志. 1989. *Tang mo Wudai sanwen yanjiu* 唐末五代散文研究 [Studies in the Prose Literature of the End Tang and the Five Dynasties]. Taiwan xuesheng shuju.

Mather, Richard B. 2002. *Shih-Shuo Hsin-Yü: A New Account of Tales of the World*. 2nd ed. University of Michigan, Center for Chinese Studies.

Müller, Gotelind. 2001. *China, Kropotkin und der Anarchismus: Eine Kulturbewegung im China des frühen 20. Jahrhunderts unter dem Einfluss des Westens und japanischer Vorbilder* [China, Kropotkin, and Anarchism: An Early Twentieth-Century Chinese Cultural Movement Influenced by the West and Japanese Examples]. Otto Harrassowitz.

Needham, Joseph. 1956. *Science and Civilisation in China*. Vol. II. Cambridge University Press.

Nienhauser, William H., Jr., ed. 1986. *The Indiana Companion to Traditional Chinese Literature*. Indiana University Press.

Nienhauser, William H., Jr., ed. 1994–2019. *The Grand Scribe's Records*. 11 vols. Indiana University Press.

Owen, Stephen. 1975. *The Poetry of Meng Chiao and Han Yü*. Yale University Press.

Owen, Stephen and Wendy Swartz, trans. 2017. *The Poetry of Ruan Ji and Xi Kang*. De Gruyter.

Peterson, C. A. 1979. "Court and province in mid- and late Tang." In *The Cambridge History of China*, vol. 3, edited by Denis Twitchett, 464–560. Cambridge University Press.

Pines, Yuri. 2014. Review of *Daoism and Anarchism* by John A. Rapp. *China Review International* 19 (3): 381–386.

Pregadio, Fabrizio, ed. 2008. *The Routledge Encyclopedia of Taoism*. Routledge.

Pregadio, Fabrizio. 2014. "Destiny, Vital Force, or Existence? On the Meanings of *Ming* in Daoist Internal Alchemy and Its Relation to *Xing* or Human Nature." *Daoism: Religion, History and Society* 6: 157–218.

Puett, Michael. 1998. "Sages, Ministers, and Rebels: Narratives from Early China Concerning the Initial Creation of the State." *Harvard Journal of Asiatic Studies* 58 (2): 425–479.

Rapp, John A. 1978. "Taoism and Anarchy: An Analysis of the Political Critique in Philosophical Taoism And Its Comparison with the Western Philosophy of Anarchism." Masters Thesis, Indiana University.

Robinet, Isabelle. 1983. "Kouo Siang ou le monde comme absolu" [Guo Xiang or the World as Absolute]. *T'oung Pao* 69: 73–107.

Robinet, Isabelle. 1986. "La notion de *hsing* dans le taoïsme et son rapport avec celle du confucianisme" [The Concept of *xing* in Daoism and its Relation to that in Confucianism]. *Journal of the American Oriental Society* 106 (1): 183–196.

Sa Mengwu 薩孟武. 1969. *Zhongguo zhengzhi sixiang shi* 中國政治思想史 [A History of Chinese Political Thought]. Sanmin shuju.

Schipper, Kristofer. 2001. "Daoist Ecology: The Inner Transformation. A Study of the Precepts of the Early Daoist Ecclesia." In *Daoism and Ecology: Ways within a Cosmic Landscape*, edited by N. J. Girardot, James Miller, and Liu Xiaogan, 79–93. Harvard University Press.

Schipper, Kristofer and Franciscus Verellen, eds. 2004. *The Taoist Canon: A Historical Companion to the Daozang*. The University of Chicago Press.

Sima Guang 司馬光. 1976. *Zizhi tongjian* 資治通鑑 [Comprehensive Mirror in Aid of Governance]. Zhonghua shuju.

Sima Qian 司馬遷. 1972. *Shiji* 史記 [Records of the Historian]. Zhonghua shuju.

Slingerland, Edward. 2014. *Trying Not to Try: Ancient China, Modern Science, and the Power of Spontaneity*. Broadway Books.

Somers, Robert M. 1979. "The end of the T'ang." In *The Cambridge History of China*, vol. 3, edited by Denis Twitchett, 682–789. Cambridge University Press.

Steavu, Dominic. 2014. "Cosmogony and the Origin of Inequality: A Utopian Perspective from Taoist Sources." *The Medieval History Journal* 17 (2): 295–335.

Stein, R. A. 1963. "Remarques sur les mouvements du taoïsme politico-religieux au II*ᵉ* siècle ap. J.-C." [Remarks on Politicoreligious Daoist Movements in the Second century CE]. *T'oung Pao* 50: 1–78.

Tackett, Nicolas. 2016. *The Destruction of the Medieval Chinese Aristocracy*. Harvard-Yenching Institute.

Torrey, Bradford, ed. 1906. *The Writings of Henry David Thoreau. Journal XIII. December 1, 1859-July 31, 1860*. Houghton Mifflin.

Twitchett, Denis, ed. 1979. *The Cambridge History of China*. Vol. 3, Part I: *Sui and T'ang China, 589-906*. Cambridge University Press.

Van der Loon, Piet. 1984. *Taoist Books in the Libraries of the Sung Period*. Ithaca Press.

Vervoorn, Aat. 1983. "Boyi and Shuqi: Worthy Men of Old?" *Papers in Far Eastern History* 28: 1–22.

Vervoorn, Aat. 1990. *Men of the Cliffs and Caves: The Development of the Chinese Eremitic Tradition to the End of the Han Dynasty*. Chinese University Press.

Wang, Richard G. 2012. *The Ming Prince and Daoism: Institutional Patronage of an Elite*. Oxford University Press.

Wang Yousan 王友三. 1982. *Zhongguo wushenlun shigang* 中國無神論史綱 [A Historical Outline of Chinese Atheism]. Renmin chubanshe.

Watson, Burton, trans. 1968. *The Complete Works of Chuang Tzu*. Columbia University Press.

Watson, Burton, trans. 1990. "*Hou Han shu*: Biographies of Recluses." *Renditions* 33–34: 35–51.

Watson, Burton, trans. 1993. *Records of the Grand Historian: Han Dynasty I*. Renditions–Columbia University Press.

Wieger, Léon. 1911. *Taoïsme. Tome 1. Bibliographie générale* [Daoism. Volume 1. General Bibliography]. Ho-kien-fu.

Xiao Gongquan 蕭公權 (K. C. Hsiao). 1966. *Zhongguo zhengzhi sixiang shi* 中國政治思想史 [A History of Chinese Political Thought]. 2nd edition. Zhonghua dadian bianyinhui.

Xu Zhen'e 徐震堮, ed. 1984. *Shishuo xinyu jiaojian* 世說新語校箋 [A New Account of Tales of the World, with Textual Criticism]. Zhonghua shuju.

Yang Bojun 楊伯峻, ed. 1985. *Liezi jishi* 列子集釋 [*Liezi* with Collected Commentaries]. Zhonghua shuju.

Yang Mingzhao 楊明照, ed. 1997. *Baopuzi waipian jiaojian* 抱朴子外篇校箋 [The Master Who Embraces Simplicity, Outer Chapters, with Textual Criticism]. Vol. 2. Zhonghua shuju.

Yu Shiyi. 2000. *Reading the* Chuang-tzu *in the T'ang Dynasty: The Commentary of Ch'eng Hsüan-ying (fl. 631–652)*. Peter Lang.

Yuan Ke 袁珂, ed. 1983. *Shanhaijing jiaozhu* 山海經校注 [Classic of Mountains and Seas with Textual Criticism and Annotation]. Shanghai guji chubanshe.

Zarrow, Peter. 1990. *Anarchism and Chinese Political Culture.* Columbia University Press.

Zhang Jinjian 張金鑑. 1989. *Zhongguo zhengzhi sixiang shi* 中國政治思想史 [A History of Chinese Political Thought]. Sanmin shuju.

Zhu Yueli 朱越利. 1982. "*Qi qi* er zi yitong bian" 炁氣二字異同辨 [On distinguishing the similarities and differences between the two characters *qi* and *qi*.]. *Shijie zongjiao yanjiu* 世界宗教研究 1: 50–58.

Ziporyn, Brook, trans. 2020. *Zhuangzi: The Complete Writings.* Hackett.